LEGENDS OF HAWAII

LEGENDS
OF
HAWAII
BY
PADRAIC COLUM

WITH DECORATIONS BY DON FORRER

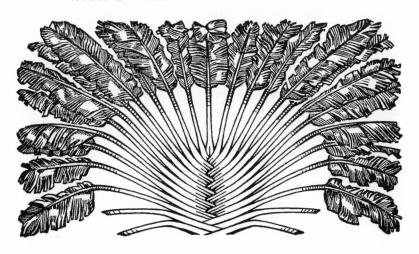

NEW HAVEN AND LONDON: YALE UNIVERSITY PRESS

Library of Congress catalog card number: 86–51288
International Standard book numbers: 0–300–00376–5 (cloth)
0–300–03923–9 (pbk.)

The paper in this book meets the guidelines for permanence
and durability of the Committee on Production Guidelines
for Book Longevity of the Council on Library Resources.

23   22   21   20   19   18   17   16   15   14

I dedicate this book to

Pardon me, noble chiefs and lineages,
For the searching place is now far and difficult;
The old plantations once scattered on the roads
Have now quite disappeared and gone with them their generation,
But although they now lie in very thick bush,
Search will be made at any rate
For Touiafutuna, the first rock
Where our origin began.
Though these are only traditions and fables
'Tis here the inquirers get their facts.

TONGAN VERSE.

THE AMASA STONE MATHER
MEMORIAL PUBLICATION FUND

The present volume is the eighteenth work published by
the Yale University Press on the Amasa Stone Mather
Memorial Publication Fund. This Foundation was estab-
lished August 25, 1922, by a gift to Yale University from
Samuel Mather, Esq., of Cleveland, Ohio, in pursuance
of a pledge made in June, 1922, on the fifteenth anniver-
sary of the graduation of his son, Amasa Stone Mather,
who was born in Cleveland on August 20, 1884, and was
graduated from Yale College in the Class of 1907. Subse-
quently, after traveling abroad, he returned to Cleveland,
where he soon won a recognized position in the business life
of the city and where he actively interested himself also in
the work of many organizations devoted to the betterment
of the community and to the welfare of the nation. His
death from pneumonia on February 9, 1920, was undoubtedly hastened by his characteristic unwillingness ever to
spare himself, even when ill, in the discharge of his duties
or in his efforts to protect and further the interests com-
mitted to his care by his associates.

PREFACE

ONE rainy day in Honolulu I went into the Bishop Museum in search of some object or record that might, like a clue, bring me to a center of Hawaiian tradition: there I was presented with volumes published by the Museum—the large, paper-covered volumes that are the Fornander Collection of Hawaiian Antiquities and Folk-lore. So voluminous was the material that it took me weeks to peruse it. The very mass of the Antiquities and Folk-lore helped to break down my present-age prepossessions, making it possible for me to get on terms with those I was reading about, people whose culture was without metals, pottery or the loom, without the horse, the cow or the sheep, whose implements were neolithic, and yet who showed a subtility of feeling that put them beside the advanced people of the high civilizations. When I had worked my way through, the names in Hawaiian tradition, the Hawaiian patterns of mind, were more or less familiar to me. And as I lived day by day with the men and women shown in the Antiquities and Folk-lore, people whose language seemed to be some Caucasian dialect made infantile (the inordinately short and the inordinately long Hawaiian words were on pages opposite the English translations, and I was taking lessons in the language every day), a way of thinking and behaving, a landscape, a history that I thought could never be comprehended by one who had not spent a lifetime on the islands began to have significance for me. . . . But now it may be asked (A) Why were Hawaiian traditions any concern of mine, and (B) What was the history and purpose of the collection of Antiquities and Folk-lore that had such impact upon me?

An answer to the second leads easily to an answer to the first. The man whose name is borne by the collection, Abraham Fornander, lived in the islands for over forty years. He edited a journal called *The Polynesian* and was once Superintendent of

Public Instruction. Married to an Hawaiian lady, he was a strong partisan of the native race. He had a theory about Polynesian migrations, the rightness or wrongness of which we need not take into account now: the important thing is that in order to substantiate it, he made an appeal to the traditions that were then current amongst the natives of Hawaii.

That was over fifty years ago. At that time there was considerable native scholarship. Haleole, who made an attempt to found a native literature with his romance *Laiekawai*, was writing and publishing. The Mission School in Lahaina-luna on the Island of Maui had become a sort of Hawaiian university. Abraham Fornander had the good sense to call on native scholars, and he was able to get the best of them to interest themselves in his project of collecting all the native lore that could throw a light on the migrations of the Polynesian people. The Hawaiian monarchy was then in undisputed existence; native institutions were still vigorous; everywhere there were men and women whose memories were stocked with the historical traditions and the romances and legends of Hawaii.

With the help of a corps of native scholars a great deal of the surviving tradition of Hawaii was collected by Fornander. Some of it was published in the Hawaiian newspapers of the time, but no extensive publication was given to it. The manuscripts were kept together; then, on the death of Abraham Fornander in 1887, the collection was acquired by Charles R. Bishop, the husband of Bernice Pauahi, an Hawaiian royalty, whose estate went to the foundation of the Bernice Pauahi Bishop Museum of Polynesian Ethnology and Natural History in Honolulu.

Forty years after it had been put together, the publication of the material was begun by the Bishop Museum. That was in 1916. The volumes appeared under the editorship of Mr. Thomas Thrumm, with the Hawaiian text on one page and the English translation by Mr. John Wise on the other. And this was the cause of my concern with Polynesian tradition. For the

Hawaiian Legislature formed a Commission on Myth and Folk-lore; the function of the Commission was to have a survey made of the stories that belonged to the myth and folk-lore of the islands, and to have them made over into stories for children—primarily for the children of the Hawaiian Islands. I was invited to make the survey and to reshape the stories.

The Fornander Collection is described as folk-lore, but I doubted from the time of my first reading of it that, speaking generally, the stories it contains are folk-lore in the strict sense of the word; I doubted their coming out of an unlearned and popular tradition. The greater number of them seemed to me to be deliberate compositions intended for a rather select audience. And then I learned that a great master of Hawaiian tradition, Mr. William Hyde Rice, favored this opinion. He speaks of bards and storytellers, either itinerant or attached to the courts of chiefs and kings, and says, "these men formed a distinct class, and lived at the courts of the high chiefs. Accordingly, their stories were heard by none except those people attached to the service of the chiefs. . . . These trained men received through their ears as we receive through our eyes, and in that way the ancient Hawaiians had a spoken literature as we have a written one." And Dr. Nathaniel Emerson speaks of "the unwritten literature of Hawaii." But what is Hawaiian is a localization of what belongs to the wider Polynesian area. Says Miss Martha Warren Beckwith, "We find the same story told in New Zealand and Hawaii scarcely changed, even in name."

In Hawaii as in the larger Polynesian area we find romance that is based on formulæ that are not familiar to us. There are practically no animal stories for the sufficient reason that the Polynesians did not have opportunities for forming a wide animal acquaintanceship. They brought the pig and the dog to the islands with them; the shark and the turtle, the owl, the rat, and the plover were the only other creatures that aroused any interest—they and the mysterious creature the Hawaiians name

'Mo-o,' a reptilian creature reminiscent, it may be, of some great lizard of the Asiatic mainland. And, speaking of the distinctiveness of these stories, it is worth while noting that the way of counting things is changed when we get into Polynesian romance: instead of three, seven, nine, we have four, eight and sixteen as cabalistic numbers. And yet, as all human desire is the same, and as human mentality compels a certain sequence of incident, and as there seem to be patterns in incident that all human beings find it delightful to work out, the Hawaiian stories have the elements and combination of elements that make for familiar narrative. Thus, in this volume, the Daughter of the King of Ku-ai-he-lani will recall Cinderella, and the story of Au-ke-le will recall stories of men who traveled far and came back to their own land after a long absence: it will remind us of Odysseus, or Rip Van Winkle, or the Gaelic hero Oisin.

In the folk-tales and the mythological romances of Europe there are places that may not be entered and there are women whom one must not approach. There is Blue Beard's Chamber; there is Danaë in her brazen tower. Hawaiian romance has places that may not be entered and women who may not be approached by men. And it has these instances in nearly every story; indeed, without the guarded maiden and the forbidden place the Hawaiian storyteller would find it difficult to carry on. And one knows that when he was dealing with one or the other of them he was dealing with the life around him: the place was *tapu*, the woman was tapu. And the place or woman was tapu simply because a chief with the privilege of declaring tapu had so declared it. And when we read one of these stories we can easily see how, as the simplicity of tapu was forgotten, the woman would be given a fantastic security like Danaë in her brazen tower, or like the Celtic Eithlinn on her inaccessible island, and we can see motives for keeping the women apart: Danaë's son and Eithlinn's son are destined to slay their grandfathers. Every race has had tapu. But the Polynesians made it their single discipline. In these Hawaiian stories we are at the beginning of romance that for Europeans became fraught with all that was unexplainable.

Something else has to be noted about these stories. Miss Beckwith thinks that the greater part of Polynesian romance is about demigods—beings descended from the gods or adopted or endowed by them. These tales, however, reflect actual conditions. "Gods and men are, in fact, to the Polynesian mind, one family under different forms, the gods having superior control over certain phenomena, a control which they can impart to their offspring on earth. . . . The supernatural blends with the natural in exactly the same way as to the Polynesian mind gods relate themselves to men, facts about one being regarded as, even though removed to the heavens, quite as objective as those which belong to the other, and being employed to explain social customs and physical appearances in actual experience."

And now about my own part in the work promoted by the Commission on Myth and Folk-lore. I went to the Hawaiian Islands in 1923. I learned something of the language; I went through the islands seeking out people who still had the tradition of Hawaiian romance and who could relate it in the traditional way; I placed myself in the hands of the very distinguished group of Polynesian scholars in Honolulu; I made a study of all the material that had been collected. Though I have dwelt on the impression that the Fornander Collection made on me, I did not draw the larger part of my material from it; I went to several other sources: what the Fornander Collection did was familiarize me as no briefer accounts could have done with the nature and extent of the Hawaiian tradition. And though I have noted the fact that the great part of the traditions that have been collected are literature rather than folk-lore in the strict sense, a large part of what I worked over is folk-lore. The old stories are long, and to us who are not in the presence of the Hawaiian storyteller with his dramatically entertaining gesture, monotonous: I had, in dealing with them, to condense, expand, heighten, subdue, rearrange—in a word, I had to retell them using the old stories as material for new wonder stories. With a few exceptions the stories I retold are Hawaiian in the sense that they were given shape on the Hawaiian Islands. One of the exceptions is "The Seven Great Deeds of Ma-ui": although the scene of the demigods' adventures is Hawaiian, I used incidents related of him in other Polynesian Islands—in New Zealand, Samoa, and the lesser islands; I have treated Ma-ui as the pan-Polynesian hero he is. The other story from outside Hawaii that is given here is "The Canoe of Rata"; it belongs to a cycle about the hero who is named Laka in Hawaii. It remains to be said that the stories given in the present volume are selections from two volumes published immediately after I had been in the Hawaiian Islands, *At the Gateways of the Day* and *The Bright Islands*. But some important stories that did not appear in the other volumes are given here.

These stories are of different types: some are folk-tales, stories told to and by unlearned people from time immemorial, and some are stories told by learned men to a cultivated audience, court romances comparable, although they are not in verse, to the lays made by minstrels for the medieval courts of Europe. The story that this collection begins with—"The Princess of the Rainbow," is actually "literary"—founded on mythical material, it was worked up into a long romance by Haleole, an Hawaiian writer of fifty years ago. I place this romance in the forefront because to me there is in it much that is symbolic. For Laie lives where the rainbow arches; scarlet birds shake the dew from the red lehua blossoms upon her head. She is hidden and guarded. So the Polynesian soul might be represented. It is hidden and guarded. It is significant that the one Polynesian word that has become general in European languages is the one that we write "taboo"—*tapu*, consecrated, given into the gods'

keeping. In Polynesian life and history there is something
guarded as Laie is guarded, something kept unrevealed, something inclosed with tapu: the deeper meaning of Hawaiian
poetry is a secret; so are the burial places of the Hawaiian Kings.
I place the story about Pe-le after the story about Laie. "The
Woman of the Rainbow" represents the idyllic element that
is such a feature of Hawaiian romance, and the "Woman of the
Pit" represents the element that is its opposite—the ruthless,
sensual, devouring life of lands where the temples were for
human sacrifice. Pe-le as a personification of the volcano has
extraordinary actuality. But Pe-le as a human being reflects one
side of the Polynesian mind. Her story shows a conception of
the soul that is akin to the Egyptian one—that it is divisible,
that part of it can be here and part of it there. As regards the
after-world, the Polynesian belief is Babylonian rather than
Egyptian: the realm of the dead that Hi-ku goes down into in
search of Ka-we-lu is like the realm of the dead that Ishtar goes
down into in search of Thammuz—a lightless world where the
spirits have only a dim existence.

In the court romances such as "The Princess of the Rainbow,"
"Ha-le-ma-no and the Princess Kama," "Companion-in-Suffering-in-the-Glade," "The Arrow and the Swing," there is a feeling that is rare in European romance, a feeling for the beauty of
nature, for flowers and trees, for the aspect of clouds, the look
of the sea, the sight of mountains, a feeling for the beauty of the
rainbow and the waterfall. The feeling in such stories is idyllic;
the people are constantly celebrating the place of their abode or
their wandering, using the distinctive Hawaiian poetry, the
me-le of place. To be true in any measure to the originals these
stories of my retelling—not the court romances alone but the
folk-tales and the mythological stories—should have in them
the rainbow and the waterfall, the volcano, the forest, the surf
as it breaks over the reef of coral. The scene of the stories, when
it is not laid in lands that are frankly mythological, is in an

Hawaiian Arcadia. And how distinctive are the lands that the Hawaiian storytellers have discovered for us! Ku-ai-he-lani, the Country that Supports the Heavens and Pali-uli, the easeful land that the gods have since hidden. Who would not roam through these lands with those who first told of them and those who first heard of them, the gracious and vivid children of Wakea and Papa?

P. C.

New York,
  Spring, 1937.

CONTENTS

Preface   vii

The Princess of the Rainbow   1

The Fire-Goddess   25

The Seven Great Deeds of Ma-ui   38

The Me-ne-hu-ne   65

The Canoe of Laka or Rata and Those Who
    Sailed in It   77

When the Little Blond Shark Went Visiting   84

The Boy Pu-nia and the King of the Sharks   92

Owl and Rat and the Boy Who Was Good at
    Shooting Arrows   97

The Story of Mo-e Mo-e   104

Ha-le-ma-no and the Princess Kama   123

"Companion-in-Suffering-in-the-Glade"   133

The Arrow and the Swing   139

The Rolling Island   146

The Daughter of the King of Ku-ai-he-lani   158

The Woman from Lalo-hana   168

Hina, the Woman in the Moon   173

The Two Great Brothers, Ni-he-u and Kana   176

Au-ke-le the Seeker   186

Kaulu, the World's Strongest Boy   203

Notes   207

Helps to Pronunciation.

There are three simple rules which practically control Hawaiian pronunciation: (1) Pronounce each vowel. (2) Never allow a consonant to close a syllable. (3) Give the vowels the following values:

$$a = a \text{ in } father$$
$$e = ey \text{ in } they$$
$$i = i \text{ in } machine$$
$$o = o \text{ in } note$$
$$u = oo \text{ in } tool$$

THE PRINCESS OF
THE RAINBOW

FIVE sisters Ai-wohi had; they were all younger than he, and they were all named after the Mai-le vine that grows in the forests of Hawaii; they were the five Mai-le sisters. The first was named Mai-le-hai-wale. The second was named Mai-le-ka-luhea. The third was named Mai-le-lau-li'i. The fourth was named Mai-le-pa-kaha. The fifth and littlest was named Ka-hala-o-mapuana. It was in the power of each of the sisters to give herself the fragrance of the vine whose name she had.

Now his five sisters stood around him and Ai-wohi spoke to them. "What I tell you now is a secret," he said, "and none else but you, my sisters, may be told about it."

"Tell us, our brother," the five sisters implored him.

"At the rising of the Canoe-Guiding Star, I sailed to another island," he told them. "I sailed there because it was told to me that a maiden who was the most beautiful in all the islands lived there. 'See where the rainbow arches! Laie the Beautiful

is there,' a sage who came to me on that island said. Then I said,
'I will wait here until the raininess clears off and the bow dis-
appears.' After three days the raininess went, and the whole
country lay bare as I awoke one morning. But still I saw the
rainbow arching where I had seen it before. I watched until
the sun came. Still the rainbow stayed. Then said the sage to me,
'The maiden you looked for is in Pali-uli, the place appointed
by the gods for her to dwell in, and the rainbow stays always
over where she is.' I went through the forests and thickets of
tangled bush, and up the side of a high mountain. And there I
saw where she lived, she who is named Laie the Beautiful. But
when I saw her dwelling, I knew that I could not win her, for
that house of hers was a marvel: it was thatched all over with
the golden feathers of the o-o bird. So I went into my canoe and
I sailed back from that island."

Then said his sisters, "What would you have us do for you,
our brother?"

Said Ai-wohi, "I came back that I might bring you with me
to Pali-uli to help me to win Laie."

The sisters said, "At dawn let us go into your canoe and make
the journey to that island." They were pleased that he had
asked them to help him. And so at dawn, when all was ready for
sailing, Ai-wohi took his sisters, even the littlest of all, Ka-
hala-o-mapuana, and set off for the island on which is Pali-uli.
And when they reached the island they went through the forests
and through the thickets of tangled bush, and up the side of a
high mountain. A cock crowed. Ai-wohi said, "We are nearly
there now." A second cock crowed. Ai-wohi said, "We are there
now. These are her woman-guardian's cocks crowing." No
farther did he go with them. They said to each other, "Here
is Pali-uli, and now let us try to win Laie the Beautiful for our
brother."

The Five Who Were Left Behind.

THE first of the sisters who went up to the house that was

thatched all over with the feathers of the o-o bird was Mai-le-hai-wale, the eldest of the five. She went up to the door of the Princess' house. It was night then, and all within the house were sleeping.

Fragrance came to Laie in her sleep. She started up. "O Waka, O my grandmother!" she cried out.

"Why do you waken me in the middle of the night?" her grandmother said.

"A fragrance has come in from the night, a strange fragrance, a cool fragrance, a fragrance that goes to my heart. I will open the door to what is there."

"The fragrance is from a girl named Mai-le-hai-wale," said her grandmother. "She has come here to get you for a wife for her brother Ai-wohi."

"I will not marry him; I will live in Pali-uli alone," said the Princess.

Mai-le-hai-wale heard what was said; she went back to her brother. He said, "If the first-born has failed, the others, no doubt, will be worthless." Then the second sister, Mai-le-ka-luhea came to him. She begged her brother to let her try to win the Princess for him.

She, the second one, went to the house. She stood at the door. The Princess wakened, feeling that fragrance. "O Waka, O my grandmother!" she cried out.

"Why do you break my sleep again in the middle of the night?"

"Here is a fragrance, a fragrance stranger than the fragrance before, a fragrance that goes to my heart."

"It is Mai-le-ka-luhea. She has come to try to win you for her brother."

"I will not open the door to her; I will not wed her brother; I will live alone in Pali-uli," the Princess said.

Then Mai-le-ka-luhea went back to her brother. "I have failed to come to the Princess," she said. "Two of us have failed. but three remain to you."

"And I," said the third sister, "will go to the house and try to win the Princess for you, my brother."

So to the house that was thatched all over with the feathers of the o-o bird Mai-le-lau-li'i went. She stood outside the door, and the fragrance went within the house. Again the Princess awakened. "O Waka, O my grandmother!" she said.

"Why do you awaken me?" said her grandmother.

"Here is a fragrance, a fragrance from a strange forest; here is a fragrance that lies around my heart."

"It is only Mai-le-lau-li'i come to try to win you for her brother," Waka said.

"I will not wed him, but will live here alone in Pali-uli."

Then Mai-le-lau-li'i went back to her brother. She was sorrowful because she had not been able to win to the Princess. Ai-wohi was angry with his sisters now; he spoke to them harshly. And then, without waiting for her brother's permission, the fourth sister, Mai-le-pa-kaha, went and stood at the door of Laie's house.

"What is this?" said the Princess when she wakened up. "This is a strange fragrance, a pleasant fragrance, a fragrance that I should like to keep around my heart."

"It is Mai-le-pa-kaha come to try to win you for her brother," said her grandmother.

"I will not wed him; she may go away," said the Princess.

When Mai-le-pa-kaha went back to him, her brother said: "Ye have been useless to me; ye have brought refusals on me that have shamed me. Stay in the jungle here, for I will not bring you back with me."

Then the four sisters began to lament. But the littlest of the sisters, young Ka-hala-o-mapuana said, "Had we known that you were bringing us to leave us in this place we never should have come with you. And now you are going away from us without giving me, the youngest sister, the chance of winning Laie the Beautiful for you. I might have won to her, my brother."

"Four refusals are enough without having a fifth one," said the unworthy Prince. "But as for you, my youngest sister, you shall come back with me."

"I will not go," said the littlest of the sisters. "I will not go with you unless we all go back to our own land together."

Then said Ai-wohi to his youngest sister: "Stay then with your sisters. All of you have been useless to me, and now you may all go wherever you wish. But I will not bring you back with me."

Ai-wohi departed, going down the side of the mountain to the place where his canoe was, and leaving his sisters there in the forest. He left them although Ka-hala-o-mapuana, the littlest of his sisters, lifted up her voice and sang to him:

"Our brother and our lord,
  Highest and closest!
  Where are you, oh, where?
  You and we, here and there—
  You, the wayfarer,
  We, the followers
  Along the cliffs, swimming around the steeps.
    No longer are we beloved.
  Do you no longer love us,
  The comrades who followed you over the Ocean,
  Over the great waves, the little waves,
  Over the long waves, the short waves,
  Over the long-backed waves of the Ocean;
  Comrades who followed you inland,
  Far through the jungle?
  Oh, turn, turn back!
  Oh, turn back and have pity!
  Listen to my pleading,
    Me, the littlest of your sisters!
  Why will you leave us forsaken
  In this desolation?

You were the one who came first—
You opened the way for us,
And we followed after you.
We are your little sisters.
    Then forsake your anger,
The wrath, the loveless heart,
Give a kiss to your little ones!
Fare you well!"

But Ai-wohi would not turn back for her singing. He went down the mountain. He came to where his canoe was, and he sailed back across the water.

How the Littlest of the Five Sisters Won to the Princess.

THE five Mai-le sisters, abandoned by their brother, lived in the forest around Pali-uli, eating berries and living in hollow trees; at night they used to light fires and sit around them, singing to each other. All day one or another of them watched for sight of the Princess, but none of them ever saw her come out of her house.

One day her elder sisters said to Ka-hala-o-mapuana, the littlest of the sisters: "All of us have tried to come to the Princess, to see her and to speak to her, except you, our youngest sister. It is for you now to think of some way of coming to her, so that we may have her protection—we who are now forsaken in this wilderness."

When this was said to her the littlest sister took the wide leaf of the ti plant, and she made a trumpet out of the leaf, and that night as she sat by the fire with her sisters she blew upon the trumpet, making merry sounds. She played, and the Princess in her house that was covered with the feathers of the o-o bird heard the music. She called to her hunchbacked attendant, and she bade her go and find out who was playing this new and strange music.

The hunchbacked attendant went out. When she came back she said to the Princess: "I went to where fires were lighted, and I saw girls around the fires—five girls, each as beautiful as any girl I ever saw. I watched them without being seen myself. One, the littlest girl, made the music, playing on an instrument of leaf with her mouth." The Princess said, "Go and bring the littlest girl to me, that she may amuse me by playing on that instrument."

So the hunchbacked attendant went again to where the fires were lighted, and she showed herself to the girls. "I have come to take the littlest girl to visit the Princess," she said, "for this the Princess has commanded."

Then Ka-hala-o-mapuana stood up and she went with the attendant; she took with her the ti-leaf trumpet, and she said good-bye to her sisters, leaving them by the fires.

And so the littlest sister came before the house that was thatched all over with the feathers of the o-o bird, the house that had not been opened to her sisters or to her brother. The door was opened for her, and she looked within. And there she saw Laie the Beautiful. She was resting upon the wings of birds. Two scarlet i'iwi birds were perched upon the shoulders of the Princess; they shook the dew from the red lehua blossoms upon her head. That sight was so marvelous to her that little Ka-hala-o-mapuana fell to the ground with a heart all shaken.

Then the Princess' attendant raised her up. But the girl said, "Permit me to return to my sisters, for the nature of your mistress is so marvelous that I am made to tremble with fear before her." The attendant said: "Have no fear. Go to the Princess as she has commanded you."

The Princess had heard their low voices; now she called to the attendant to bring Ka-hala-o-mapuana to her. Then the girl came within the house and stood before Laie the Beautiful.

Said Laie, looking at what the girl held in her hand, "Is this the instrument that I heard sounded?"

"Yes, Princess," said the girl, "and the instrument is mine."

Then said Laie, "Play upon it, so that I may hear the merry sounds again." Ka-hala-o-mapuana put the ti-leaf trumpet to her mouth and played upon it, and Laie was delighted with the music that she made. The Princess had never heard an instrument of that kind sounded before, and she had Ka-hala-o-mapuana play again and again for her. She tried to play on it herself, but she was not able to make any sound come from the leaf. Then she said, "Let us two be friends; you shall live here in my house and make music for me."

Then said the littlest of the Mai-le sisters: "I am happy that you should ask me to play to you. But I have sisters, and they have already been forsaken, and I cannot forsake them."

Laie asked her how she had come to that place with her sisters, and Ka-hala-o-mapuana told her of how they had been brought there by their brother, and told her all that had happened. She told her, too, the names of her four sisters, and Laie knew that they were the girls who had come to the door of her house, and whose fragrance had come to her. Their brother was now gone from the place, and she thought she might let the girls stay for the sake of the merry music that the littlest of them made. She would have a house built for them, she said, and she would give the five girls her protection. Then, in great joy, the littlest of the Mai-le sisters went back to where her sisters were seated around the fires.

She told them that the Princess had commanded them all to appear before her. They, too, rejoiced. They left the hollow trees where they had been living the lives of the forsaken, and went to the Princess' house.

When the attendant opened the door and when the four girls saw Laie the Beautiful resting on the wings of birds with the scarlet birds shaking the dew from the lehua blossoms upon her head, their hearts trembled because of the marvel of that sight, and they fell upon the ground. Ka-hala-o-mapuana went toward the Princess. Then Laie spoke to them kindly, and when they came and stood near her, she said:

"I have heard that you are all sisters, and so I would have you live together in one house; and whatever one says, that the other shall do." To this the five girls agreed, and the youngest sister said:

"Princess, we are happy that you have received us, and all five of us will become a guard for your house." The Princess agreed to let this be, and she made the Mai-le sisters guards over the whole of Pali-uli. No one might come to the Princess unless he or she was brought to her by the Mai-le sisters.

Thus the five sisters dwelt in Pali-uli, and all the time they were there it seemed to them that every day was happier for them than the day that had passed. Not for an hour did they ever weary of life. Food was brought to them, but they never looked on the person who had made it ready. Birds fetched what they ate to them, and cleared away all that was left over. Pali-uli became for the sisters a land beloved; they watched over the Princess and guarded the house that was thatched all over with the feathers of the o-o bird—the house that the rainbow arched above, and that had the strange Mo-o to guard it. And now their only fear was that their brother would come back and try once more to gain the Princess, Laie the Beautiful.

Ai-wohi Returns to Pali-uli.

As for Ai-wohi, the unworthy Prince, he went sailing over the water to his own country. But he did not reach his own country on that voyage; he was drawn to another island by a woman whom he saw seated upon a cliff.

It was one of his steersmen who saw the woman first. The man called out and spoke about her beauty, and when Ai-wohi looked he saw that the woman was beautiful indeed. He asked who she was, and the steersmen told him that she was the Woman of the Mountain, and that her name was Poli-ahu, Cloak of Cold.

So Ai-wohi had the canoe go to where she was. When they came near she rose up in her beautiful cloak and spoke to them. "O Poli-ahu, princess of the cliff and mistress of the coast," said Ai-wohi, "we are well met indeed."

"I am not the mistress of the coast," said the fair woman to him. "I am come from the summit of the mountain. Look! it is clothed in a white garment like the one I wear."

They talked together, and Ai-wohi thought that if he could win this fair woman to be his bride he might be able to forget about Laie the Beautiful. He asked her to be his wife, and she consented. He knelt before her and he gave her the beautiful feather cape that he had brought for the Princess of Pali-uli. She threw over him the cloak that she wore, her cloak of dazzling whiteness. She promised, too, that she would come to the house that he would be in.

To that house she came. All wondered to see that strange white woman there. But all who had met for sport and dancing shivered when the Woman of the Mountain came amongst them, for the cold came with her. Ai-wohi led her back, and up to her mountain summit, and there he nearly died of the cold. He came back to where his companions were, and his heart was the more filled with longing for Laie, the Princess who lived in the house that was thatched all over with the feathers of the o-o bird, the house that the rainbow arched above.

Then one came to him who spoke of the beauty of the Princess, and who told him of the five young girls who guarded Pali-uli. When Ai-wohi heard of these guards he said to himself: "These are my sisters. How lucky it is that I left them behind! Everything in Pali-uli is now in their charge. They will not prevent my going into the Princess' house." Then he went into his canoe, and with his companions he returned to Pali-uli for the third time.

He went for a monstrous dog that he owned—Ka-la-hu-moku, the devouring dog from Tahiti. No man or company of men could face this dog. Ai-wohi thought that even if his sisters did not let him go into the Princess' house his monstrous dog would overcome them and leave Pali-uli without guards, so that he could force Laie the Beautiful to come with him. When he thought of all this he did not know of the great creature that guarded Pali-uli—the great Mo'o that was named Kiha-nui-lulu-moku.

He left his monstrous dog in a cave near where he landed, and once again he climbed up to Pali-uli. He thought he would come to the Princess without his sisters holding him back. He went on until he came to the first of the Princess' guardians.

This was Mai-le-hai-wale. She knew him, and she wept when she saw him, remembering how loving she had been to him in their parents' house, and remembering how he had forsaken her and her sisters in this strange place. She said: "You have no right to come up here; I am the outpost of the Princess' guards, and it is my business to drive all back who come up here; turn back then, turn back without delay."

But Ai-wohi did not turn back. He spoke to Mai-le-hai-wale, and he won past her, and he went on. And then he came to the second of the Princess' guards, to Mai-le-ka-luhea, who was now before him.

Said Mai-le-ka-luhea, knowing her brother: "How is this! You abandoned us, and now you come here again. But now we are the Princess' guards, and we cannot let you go past."

Said Ai-wohi, "I am here only to look at the Princess' house." Then he made Mai-le-ka-luhea remember the love that she had had for him, and he won past the place she guarded, and he went on.

And then he came to the third guard, to Mai-le-lau-li'i. Her, too, Ai-wohi persuaded, and she let him pass. And then he came to the fourth guardian, to Mai-le-pa-kaha, and her he made weep by speaking to her about their life together in their parents' house. He went past her, and he came in sight of the house that was thatched all over with the feathers of the o-o bird.

And there he came upon the littlest of his sisters, upon Ka-hala-o-mapuana, who was on guard before the house. When she saw her brother she became very angry, and she cried out: "Hasten back! You have no business here. If you do not go back, I will call on the birds of Pali-uli, and they will pick the flesh off your bones." He spoke to her then, calling her the youngest and dearest of his sisters. But still she cried out: "Return at once, delay not your going. We now protect the Princess who protected us when you abandoned us." Ai-wohi knew that he could not move this guard nor win past her. He swore vengeance against her, but she called to the birds of Pali-uli, and they flew toward him and made a cloud about his head. Then Ai-wohi went back once more from Pali-uli.

How Ai-wohi Cheated the Princess.

HE brought out of the cave the monstrous dog from Tahiti— the dog Ka-la-hu-moku—and he bade him go and destroy his five sisters and destroy all the guardians of Pali-uli, and carry off Laie the Beautiful and bring her to him in the cave. The monstrous dog bounded off to do as his master bade him. And Ai-wohi sent too his two bird messengers, Snipe and Turnstone, to bring back word to him about how the dog fared.

Now the youngest of the five Mai-le sisters began to fear for what her brother might do, and she went to the great Mo'o that guarded Pali-uli—to the great Mo'o that was terrible when awake, but that slept nearly all the time. She wakened up the Mo'o, and she said to him: "O Kiha-nui-lulu-moku, O our guardian! Sleep no more, but guard us and guard Pali-uli. Guard us from this lawless man, this mischief-maker, this rogue from the sea who is my brother! Guard us, O great Mo'o." Then the Mo'o wakened up in every bit of his dragon-length, and prepared to guard Pali-uli.

It was just then that Ai-wohi's bird messengers came in advance of the great dog from Tahiti. They heard a humming in the thickets. They did not know what this humming was, but it was the tongue of the great Mo'o going here and going there. They did not see the great Mo'o. But as they flew on they knew that there was something above them. It was the upper jaw of the great Mo'o, for his mouth was now open and one part of it touched the ground and one part of it was high above where they flew. The birds were nearly caught between the great Mo'o's jaws. They flew out in time to save themselves. Then they flew high in the air, and they saw below them the great guardian of Pali-uli. They knew that it was only by the quickness of their flight that they had escaped.

Then they saw Ka-la-hu-moku, the monstrous dog from Tahiti, racing toward Pali-uli. As the dog came near, the Mo'o sniffed, and with that sniff he nearly drew the birds down through the air. The great dog came along, and he was faced by the great Mo'o. The dog showed his rows of teeth. But with one snap of his jaws the Mo'o took off an ear and took off the tail of the dog. The howl that came from Ka-la-hu-moku was heard down in the cave where Ai-wohi stayed. Then the dog turned and went from Pali-uli.

And when Ai-wohi saw his monstrous dog all disfigured he hardened his heart and he swore he would not go from Pali-uli until he had his revenge for this defeat. He bade his bird messengers stay around Pali-uli and tell him of all that was happening there.

And that day Ai-wohi's bird messengers heard Waka, Laie's

grandmother, speak to her. What the bird messengers heard her say, that they brought straight to Ai-wohi.

Waka said to her granddaughter: "The time has come when you are to be given to the husband that I have chosen for you. Tomorrow he will come. The birds will carry you on their wings down to the beach. I will cause a mist to come down, a mist that will hide you from all the people there. And you will take your surfboard and ride on the crested waves. When the mist clears you will see one near you. He is the man who will be your husband. Go on your board with him back to the shore. You will give him a kiss there, and because you have never given a kiss to any other man he, the Prince whom I have sent for, will take you as his wife. But if you had given a kiss to another man, he would never take you. Make ready, then, to meet him tomorrow."

His bird messengers told all this to Ai-wohi. And when Ai-wohi heard the plan of Laie's grandmother he rejoiced, for he thought that a way was shown him to have revenge on those who dwelt in Pali-uli and to win Laie the Beautiful for himself.

That night while he slept he had a dream. He dreamt that he slept in a hollow tree, and that he saw a little bird building her nest just outside the tree. When the nest was built the bird that owned it flew away. By and by another bird came. This bird took the nest and stayed in it. And Ai-wohi was sure that his dream meant that Laie the Beautiful would be won, not by him for whom her grandmother had prepared her, but by himself, Ai-wohi. And with this thought in his mind he went down to the sea and took out his surfboard and went out on the waves.

Then Waka covered land and sea with a mist. And through that mist, hidden from all who were there, Laie the Beautiful came, borne on the wings of the birds of Pali-uli. She alighted on the beach; she took her surfboard and swam out with it. She was on the crested waves, stretched on her surfboard, when the mist cleared away.

And when she looked around her there were two men there. This filled her with surprise, for she looked to see only one man. Then, as she rested on her surfboard, Ai-wohi came near her. He caught her by her feet, and put an arm around her, and then her surfboard was lost in the waves. She looked around and she saw the other man—he was the Prince for whom her grandmother had prepared her—standing on his surfboard and being carried by the crested wave toward the shore.

And now Laie and Ai-wohi were swimming together in the open sea. She looked around and she said, "The land has vanished." He said: "All this is as your grandmother planned. Come upon my surfboard." Laie went upon his surfboard. A crested wave arose. They did not take it. Another crested wave arose. They did not take it. A third crested wave arose. They took this wave, and they were carried to the shore. Then they stood together, and Ai-wohi said: "How well all that your grandmother planned has come about! Here am I who am to be your husband standing beside you, and all the people on the shore are watching to see you give me your kiss." Then Laie the Beautiful kissed Ai-wohi, and all the people shouted. They thought that nothing now would bar the marriage between the Princess of Pali-uli and the most worthy of all the Islands' Princes.

How Ka-hala-o-mapuana Journeyed to the Shining Heavens.

BUT Waka looked before her, and she saw the Prince whom she had chosen for her granddaughter's husband coming up from the sea. She looked again, and she saw Laie giving a second kiss to Ai-wohi. She was angry indeed; she went swiftly to Laie and she said to her:

"This is the man you have chosen. Take him now for your husband and leave Pali-uli with him. Never again will you be permitted to live in the house that is thatched all over with the feathers of the o-o bird. Never again will you have the power to rest upon the wings of birds. I will go now to your sister Lohe-lohe, and all that I once gave to you I will give to her."

And when Waka said that to her, Laie looked on the man who was beside her, and she knew him for Ai-wohi, who had abandoned his sisters and who had tried to deceive her—who had deceived her into giving him her kisses. She ran from him and went to Waka. But Waka flung her away from her. Then Laie ran away from Waka and from Ai-wohi; as she went along the beach she saw that the Prince whom her grandmother had chosen for her was going away in his canoe.

The birds would carry her no more upon their wings. Through the brush and the jungle she made her way up to Pali-uli. But when she reached the place where the rainbow arched over the house that was thatched all over with the feathers of the o-o bird, the rainbow was not there, and the house with the o-o feathers was no longer there.

Then Laie the Beautiful sank down on the ground and wept because she was now outcast and forsaken. But as she wept the five Mai-le sisters came before her. And the youngest of the sisters, Ka-hala-o-mapuana, raised her up and spoke to her. The littlest of the maidens said:

"We became your guardians while Waka still protected you, and now that you are in trouble we will share your trouble. We will not forsake you, and do you not forsake us until death shall part us all." When Laie the Beautiful heard the words the sisters said, her tears fell down because of the love she had for her comrades. And from that time, although her beautiful house was no more, although the birds did not carry her on their wings, and although the rainbow did not arch over where she was, the Princess had good and faithful attendants.

And the great Mo'o stayed to guard Laie the Beautiful. It carried the Princess and the five Mai-le sisters to the lowlands of Olaa. There they lived, and there the five sisters built a house for the Princess and got roots and fruits for food for all of them. They heard no more of Ai-wohi, their brother, nor of Waka, Laie's grandmother.

One day the sisters came to the Princess, and the youngest of them said: "Know that we have another brother—a brother of such high rank that the place he lives in is called the Shining Heavens. He is a beautiful youth, and he is named 'Eyeball-of-the-Sun.' The way to where he is is difficult, but we have decided to go to him and to bring him to you, that you may have him for a husband and so be lifted up from the lowly state that you are in." At first the Princess would not let any of the sisters go on a journey that was so far as to the Shining Heavens. But at last she was persuaded to let the littlest of the sisters, Ka-hala-o-mapuana, go.

The great Mo'o carried the little maiden on his dragon back, and they went across the ocean, and in four months they came to the country that was near to the Shining Heavens.

When they came to that country the Watcher of the Land was away. When he came back he found the great Mo'o there. It was asleep; its head filled all the great house, and its tail was still in the sea. A terrible sight it was for the Watcher of the Land! Then Kiha-nui-lulu-moku lifted up its tail; the sea swelled, the waves rose over the cliffs, the spume of the sea rose high, and the white sand was flung upon the shore. Then the Watcher was greatly frightened. He drew back, and as he did so Ka-hala-o-mapuana appeared.

"Whose child are you?" said the Watcher.

Ka-hala-o-mapuana told him, showing him that she was related to all the great ones of the land. Then said the Watcher, "I am your uncle, and I will show you the road you must take to reach your brother who dwells in the Shining Heavens and is named 'Eyeball-of-the-Sun.'"

He called up to the sky, and the Great Spider of the Sky let down a spider web that made a network in the air. Then the

Watcher of the Land instructed Ka-hala-o-mapuana what she was to do. "Climb up this network," he said, "and when you come to the top you will find an old man with gray hair there. He is your grandfather. But if he should look upon you, he will not hear what you have to say, for he will take you for another, and you will die. But if you can come to him before he sees you, you will be able to win your way to the Shining Heavens where your brother is.

"Wait until the Gray Man is asleep. Should he turn his face down, he is not asleep. When you see him with his face turned upward he is asleep indeed. Go to him; sit down upon his breast, and hold his beard tight in your hands. Call out to him, saying this:

> "Old Gray Man, old Gray Man,
> Here am I, your child, your child:
> Grant to me sight, the long sight, the deep sight;
> Release for me the one in the heavens,
> My brother and lord.
> Awake!
> Old Gray Man, awake!

So you must call to him; and if he questions you, tell him of the errand you have come on.

"On the way up to where the Gray Man is, if the rain covers you and if the cold comes on you, do not cower. Keep up and on. And then, if a fragrance comes to you, it is from your mother; when you smell that fragrance all is well and you are near to the end of your journey. If the sun's rays pierce you and the heat strikes you, do not fear. Try to bear it. Then you will enter the land that is called the Shadow of the Moon, and you will be safe from the heat."

After the Watcher had told all this to her, Ka-hala-o-mapuana climbed up the spider's web; she went on and on, and when the evening came she was all covered with the fine rain. Still she went on. And then a fragrance came to her, and she knew that it was from where her mother was. From dawn until when the sun was high she traveled on; the heat of the sun bore down on her. She did not shrink, but kept up and on.

But she longed to reach the place that was called the Shadow of the Moon, where the heat would not be upon her. She went on, and she came into the Shadow of the Moon.

It was night there, and she saw a high house standing before her. She saw a Gray Man there whom she knew to be her grandfather. He was still awake, and she did not approach him.

She watched and watched without moving from the place she was in. Then the Gray Man's face turned upward. She knew that he was asleep; she ran quickly to where he was, and sat down on his breast and seized his beard in her hands. She called out to him the words that had been taught to her by the Watcher below.

The Gray Man awoke. His beard, in which was his strength, was held fast by Ka-hala-o-mapuana; she kept twisting it here and there until his breath was all gone. Then he said to her:

"Whose child are you?"

"Your own," she said to him.

"Mine by whom?"

"Yours by Lau-kiele-ula."

"Which of our children are you?"

"I am Ka-hala-o-mapuana, the littlest and the youngest of your children."

Said her grandfather: "Let go my beard. You are indeed my child."

She let go his beard, and her grandfather rose up and set her in his lap. Then he said, "On what errand have you come?"

"I have come on a journey to seek one in the Shining Heavens."

"To seek which one in the Shining Heavens?"

"To seek my brother who is called 'Eyeball-of-the-Sun.' "

"Him found, what to do with him?"

"To bring him to my own land to be the husband of Laie the Beautiful, the Princess of broad Hawaii."

Said her grandfather: "It is not mine to give consent to what you ask. Your mother is the only one who can give consent. Go to her in her sacred house, and ask her to let your brother and your lord become the husband of the Princess of broad Hawaii."

She went, and she came to the sacred house where her mother was. And when her mother asked her why she had come so far, Ka-hala-o-mapuana said: "I have come to get my youthful brother for a husband for our friend, the Princess of broad Hawaii, Laie the Beautiful. She protected us when we were lovelessly deserted by our elder brother. What he did has shamed us. And we have no other way of repaying the Princess for the protection she has given us than to get for her a worthier husband than the one that her grandmother had chosen for her. Permit me then, my mother, to bring our princely brother down to where she is."

Her mother said: "If anyone but you, Ka-hala-o-mapuana, had come for him, I should never have consented to let him go from the Shining Heavens and wed with one of the world's women. Since you have come, I will not hold him back. Indeed, your youthful brother has often said that the one he loves best and thinks most of is you yourself, Ka-hala-o-mapuana."

Her mother then called upon Halulu, the great bird, saying:

"O Halulu, at the edge of the light,
 O bird that covers the sun,
 O bird that holds back the clouds above,
 Here is one from the Heavens, a child of ours;
 Come, take her, take her up to Awakea, the bright Noontide."

Then Halulu, that tremendous bird, drooped down its wings while its body remained aloft, and Ka-hala-o-mapuana and her mother climbed up the wings of the bird and sat upon its body. Then the tremendous bird flew off and up, off toward the Shining Heavens, and up to where Awakea, the bright Noontide, is—Awakea, who is at the door of the Sun.

When they went so far they found that the door of the Sun was blocked by great thunderclouds. Then Lau-kiele-ula ordered Awakea to open the way to the door for them. Awakea put forth his hands, and the great clouds melted away.

Lau-kiele-ula and Ka-hala-o-mapuana went within, and they found the Prince of the Shining Heavens sleeping in his chamber. His mother caught a ray of the sun and held it, and then the Prince awakened and turned toward them.

"Oh," cried his mother, "here is your sister, your littlest sister; she has come to visit you."

The Prince of the Shining Heavens ordered the guards of the shades to come forward. And when they came, and when shadows were brought across the place where he lay, he called to his sister, and she came and stood before him.

Then the Prince of the Shining Heavens rejoiced that the littlest of his sisters had come to him, for long had been the days of their separation. Ka-hala-o-mapuana told him about Laie the Beautiful, and told him that she had come to bring him from his high place so that he might take the Princess of broad Hawaii for his wife.

And when she had told him of the Princess, her friend, he turned to his mother, and he said: "Lau-kiele-ula, it is yours to give or to withhold consent. Do you consent to my going to win the one she speaks of for my wife?"

"I have consented already," his mother told him. "But if anyone else had come to win consent, I would not consent."

Then said the Prince of the Shining Heavens: "Return, Ka-hala-o-mapuana, return to your sisters and to the Princess, your friend. My wife she will be. Listen, and I will tell you the signs of my coming to her.

"When the rains fall and flood your lands I shall still be here in the Shining Heavens; when the billows swell and the surf throws white sands upon the shore, I shall still be here; when the thunder peals without rain coming, I shall still be here.

"But when the thunder peals again and then ceases, I shall have left my house in the Shining Heavens; when the thunder rolls and the rains pour down and the ocean swells and the land is flooded, when the lightning flashes and a mist overhangs the land, when the rainbow arches and a colored cloud rests on the ocean, I shall be behind the mountain.

"Then my meeting with your Princess will come about; it will be in the dusk of the evening on which the full moon rises. Take this to give to Laie, that I may know her then—this rainbow garment."

Ka-hala-o-mapuana took the rainbow garment, and she rejoiced, knowing that she had won her brother for a husband for her friend. Out of his house they went, she and Lau-kiele-ula, and they took their seats again on the body of Halulu, and they were brought down by the tremendous bird, down to her mother's house. From there she descended by the thread that was let down for her by the Great Spider of the Sky. She came to the place where the Mo'o was, with its tail far out in the ocean. She went on the back of the Mo'o, and they went across the ocean, and after many moons she came again to the place where her sisters and the Princess stayed in broad Hawaii.

How the Prince of the Shining Heavens Came to and Went from Laie.

ALL the signs that the Prince of the Shining Heavens spoke of came to pass—thunder pealed in the sky in the dry weather and in the wet weather; rain and lightning came; the billows swelled on the ocean; the freshets flowed on the land; land and sea were covered by a mist, and a colored cloud rested on the ocean.

Then came the time of the full moon. In the early morning when the sun rose above the mountains, the Prince of the Shining Heavens was to be seen, encircled by a red mist. The Prince of the Shining Heavens looked down, and he saw the one who was clothed in the rainbow garment, and he knew her for Laie the Beautiful, the Princess of broad Hawaii, whom he was to wed. In the dusk of the evening he came down. All his sisters bowed before him; he went to Laie and took her hands.

Then he took Laie and brought her up to the land in the Shadow of the Moon. For ten days they stayed there. Then his sisters saw a rainbow being let down from the moon to the earth. Down the ladder of the rainbow came Laie and her husband.

After that the Prince of the Shining Heavens made his sisters rulers over the islands, and once again Laie and her husband went within the clouds and they dwelt in his house in the Shining Heavens.

A long time they lived there, and for a long time Laie was happy with her husband. He went often down to the earth. Once when he was away for a whole year from his house in the Shining Heavens, Laie went to the father of the Prince, and she said to him, "Give me power to see what is happening where the Prince, my husband, is."

He said to her: "Go to my wife's house. If you find that she is sleeping, go within. You will see a gourd that is plaited with straw and feathers. That is her gourd. Do not be afraid of the great birds that are on either side of it. When you come to it, take the cover off the gourd, put your head into it, and call out its name, saying, 'Lau-ka-palili, Trembling Leaf, give me vision.' You will get vision then, and you will see all that you would see. But you must speak in a low voice, for you must not awaken Lau-kiele-ula, who guards the Gourd of Vision. She guards it by night, but in the daytime she sleeps."

In the morning Laie went to Lau-kiele-ula's dwelling; she watched until she knew that Lau-kiele-ula slept. She went to where the Gourd of Vision stood, and she was not made afraid by the great birds that stood on either side of it. She lifted the cover off the gourd; she put her head within it and she called out, "Lau-ka-palili, Trembling Leaf, give me vision."

Then vision came to her; she saw all that was happening at a distance; she saw the Prince of the Shining Heavens with her sister, and she knew that Lohe-lohe, and not she, was his beloved one.

Great grief came to Laie. She was alone now in the Shining Heavens, and for a whole year she told no one what she had seen. Then she told the father and mother of the Prince. They let down the rainbow and they came to where he was. They took all his powers away from him, and never afterward was he able to go up into the Shining Heavens. He wandered about the Islands then, his place and his glory lost to him. Nor did Laie ever go back to the Shining Heavens. She found her sister Lohe-lohe, and they lived together, with the Mai-le sisters to wait upon them and guard them. And ever afterward the Princess of the Rainbow was known to the people as the Woman of the Twilight.

THE
FIRE-GODDESS

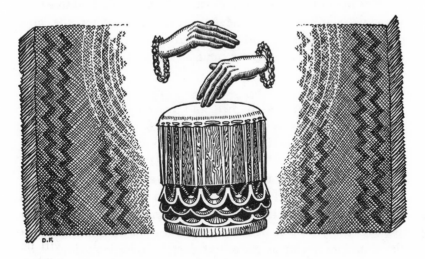

I.

PE-LE, the Goddess, came up out her pit in Ki-lau-ea. No longer would she sit on the lava hearth below, with skin rugged and blackened, with hair the color of cinders, and with reddened eyes; no longer would she seem a hag whom no man would turn toward. She came up out of the pit a most lovely woman. Her many sisters were at her side, and each of them was only less lovely than was Pe-le upon that day. They stood each side of her because it was forbidden to come behind the Goddess or to lay a hand upon her burning back.

Pe-le and her sisters stood on the crater's edge. Around them was the blackened plain, but below them was Puna, with the surf breaking upon its beach, and with its lehua groves all decked with scarlet blossoms. This land was Pe-le's. She had made it and she had the power to destroy it. She had power in the heavens, too, for her flames reached up to the skies. All the

Gods—even the great Gods, Ku, Ka-ne, Ka-ne-loa, and Lono—
were forced to follow her when she left Kahiki, the land beyond
the vastness of the ocean, and came to Hawaii. Ki-lau-ea on
Hawaii's island was the home she had chosen. And now she came
out of the pit, and she said to her many sisters, "Come, let us go
down to the beach at Puna, and bathe, and feast, and enjoy
ourselves." Her sisters rejoiced, and they went down with her
to the beach.

And when they had bathed and feasted, and had sported
themselves in the water and along the beach, Pe-le went into a
cavern and laid herself down to sleep. She said to the sister who
was always beside her, to the sister who was named Hi-i-aka-of-
the-Fire-Bloom, "Let me sleep until I awake of my own accord.
If any of you should attempt to awaken me before, it will be
death to you all. But if it has to be that one of you must awaken
me, call the youngest of our sisters, Hi-i-aka-of-the-Bosom-of-
Pe-le, and let her bring me out of sleep." So Pe-le said, and she
lay in the cavern and slept. Her sisters said to each other, "How
strange that the havoc-maker should sleep so deeply and without
a bedfellow!" By turns they kept watch over her as she slept in
the cavern.

But the youngest of her sisters was not by her when she spoke
before going to sleep. Little Hi-i-aka had gone to where the
groves of lehua showed their scarlet blossoms. She was enchanted
with the trees that she went amongst; she gathered the blossoms
and wove them into wreaths. And then she saw another girl
gathering blossoms and weaving them into wreaths and she knew
this other girl for the tree spirit, Ho-po-e. And Ho-po-e, seeing
Hi-i-aka, danced for her. These two became friends; they danced
for each other, and they played together, and never had Hi-
i-aka, the little sister of the dread Goddess, known a friend that
was as dear and as lovely as Ho-po-e whose life was in the grove
of lehuas.

As for Pe-le, the Goddess, she slept in the cavern, and in her

sleep she heard the beating of a drum. It sounded like a drum
that announces a hula. Her spirit went from where she slept; her
spirit body followed the sound of that drum. Over the sea her
spirit body followed that sound. Her spirit body went to the
Island of Kauai. There she came to a hall sacred to Laka: a hula
was being performed there. As a most lovely woman Pe-le
entered that hall. All the people who were assembled for the
hula turned to look upon her. And in that hall Pe-le saw Prince
Lo-hi-au.

He was seated on a dais, and his musicians were beside him.
Pe-le, advancing through the hall filled with wondering people,
went to where he was. Prince Lo-hi-au had her sit beside him; he
had tables spread to feast her. Pe-le would not eat. "And yet she
must have come from a very great distance," the people around
her said, "for if a woman so beautiful lived on this island, we
would surely have heard her spoken about." Prince Lo-hi-au
would not eat either; his mind was altogether on the beautiful
woman who sat on the dais beside him.

When the hula was over he took her into his house. But although they were beside each other on the mat, Pe-le would not
permit him to caress her. She let him have kisses, but kisses only.
She said to him, "When I bring you to Hawaii you shall possess
me and I shall possess you." He tried to grasp her and hold her,
but she rose in her spirit body and floated away, leaving the
house, leaving the island, crossing the sea, and coming back to
where her body lay in the cavern in Puna.

Prince Lo-hi-au sought wildly for the woman who had been
with him; he sought for her in the night, in the dark night of the
ghosts. And because it seemed to him that she was forever gone,
he went back into his house, and took his loin cloth off, and
hanged himself with it from the ridgepole of the house. In the
morning his sister and his people came in the house and found
the chieftain dead. Bitterly they bewailed him; bitterly they
cursed the woman who had been with him and who had brought

him to his death. Then they wrapped the body in robes of tapa and laid it in a cavern of the mountainside.

In Puna, in a cavern, Pe-le's body lay, seemingly in deep sleep. For a day and a night, and a night and a day it lay like this. None of her sisters dared try to awaken Pe-le. But at last they became frightened by the trance that lasted so long. They would have their youngest sister, Hi-i-aka, awaken the Woman of the Pit. At the end of another day they sent for her.

And Hi-i-aka saw the messenger coming for her as she stood in the grove of lehua trees with her dear and lovely friend, Ho-po-e, beside her. She watched the messenger coming for her, and she chanted the me-le:

> "From the forest land at Papa-lau-ahi,
> To the garlands heaped at Kua-o-ka-la,
> The lehua trees are wilted,
> Scorched, burnt up—
> Consumed are they by fire—
> By the fire of the Woman of the Pit."

But Ho-po-e, her friend, said, "It is not true what you chant. See! Our lehuas are neither wilted nor burnt up. If they were I would no longer be able to see you nor to speak with you. Why, then, do you lament? You will stay with me, and we shall gather more blossoms for garlands." But Hi-i-aka said, "Even as I saw the messenger who is coming to take me away from you, I saw our trees destroyed by Pe-le's fires."

Then the messenger came to them, and told Hi-i-aka that she was to return to where she had left her sisters. She took farewell of Ho-po-e and went to where her sisters awaited her. They brought her within the cavern, and they showed her Pe-le lying there, without color, without stir. Then Hi-i-aka, the youngest of her sisters, went to Pe-le's body and chanted over it. And the spirit body that had been hovering over the prostrate body entered into it. The breath entered the lungs again; Pe-le's bosom rose and fell; color came into her face. Then the Woman of the Pit stretched her body; she rose up, and she spoke to her sisters.

They left that place; they went back into Pe-le's dwelling place, into the pit of Ki-lau-ea. Then, after a while, Pe-le spoke to her sisters, one after the other. She said to each of them, "Will you be my messenger and fetch our lover—yours and mine—from Kauai?" None of the elder sisters would go; each one understood how dangerous such a mission would be. But when Pe-le spoke to Hi-i-aka, the youngest of her sisters, the girl said, "Yes, I will go, and I will bring back the man."

Her sisters were dismayed to hear Hi-i-aka say this. The journey was long, and for anyone who would go on the mission that Pe-le spoke of the danger was great. Who could tell what fit of rage and hatred might come over the Woman of the Pit— rage and hatred against the one who would be with the man she would have for her lover? And Hi-i-aka who had agreed to go upon such a mission was the youngest and the least experienced of all of them. They tried to warn her against going; but they dared not speak their thought out to her. Besides, they knew that Hi-i-aka was so faithful to Pe-le, her chieftainess and her elder sister, that she would face every danger at her request.

Then said Pe-le to Hi-i-aka, "When you have brought our lover here, for five days and five nights he shall be mine. After that he shall be your lover. But until I have lifted the tapu you must not touch him, you must not caress him, you must not give him a kiss. If you break this tapu it shall be death to you and to Prince Lo-hi-au." Her sisters made signs to her, and Hi-i-aka delayed her departure. She stood before Pe-le again, and Pe-le reproached her for her dilatoriness. But now Hi-i-aka spoke to her elder sister and chieftainess and said, "I go to bring a lover to you while you stay at home. But, going, I make one condition. If you must break out in fire and make raids while I am gone, raid the land that we both own, but do not raid where the lehua groves are; do not harm my friend Ho-po-e, whose life is in the lehua groves." She said this, and she started on her journey. But now the length of the journey and its dangers came before her and made her afraid. She saw herself, alone and powerless, going upon that long way. Once again she returned to where the Woman of the Pit sat. She asked that she be given a companion for the journey. She asked that a portion of Pe-le's mana, or magic power, be given her. Pe-le did not deny her this: she called upon the Sun and the Moon, the Stars, the Wind, the Rain, the Lightning, and Thunder to give aid to her sister and her messenger. And now that mana was bestowed on her, Hi-i-aka started on the way that led across islands and over seas to the house of the man whom her sister desired—her sister, Pe-le, the dread Fire-Goddess.

II.

FAR did Hi-i-aka and her woman companion journey, long were they upon the way, many dangers did they face and overcome, and at last they came to the village that had Lo-hi-au for its lord. "Why have you come?" said the people who entertained the worn travelers. "I have come to bring Prince Lo-hi-au to Pe-le, that they may be lovers." "Lo-hi-au has been dead many days. He fell under the spell of a witch, and he took his own life." Then they pointed out to her the cave in the mountainside in which his sister had laid the body of Lo-hi-au.

Then was Hi-i-aka greatly stricken. But she drew together all the power that she had—the power that Pe-le had endowed her with—and looked toward the cave in the mountainside. And she saw something hovering around the cave, and she knew it, thinned and wan as it was, for the ghost body of Lo-hi-au. She knew that she had to bring that ghost body back to the body that lay in the cave, and she knew that all the toil she had been through would be nothing to the toil that this would entail. She raised her hands toward the cave, and she uttered a chant to hold that ghost body in the place. But as she looked she saw that the ghost body was even more thinned and wan than she had thought. She was frightened by its shadowiness. The voice that came to her from before the cave was as thin and faint as the murmur that the land shell gives out. She answered it back in a voice that was filled with pity:

> "My man of the wind-driven mist,
>   Or rain that plunges clean as a diver
>   What time the mountain stream runs cold
>   Adown the steps at Ka-lalau—
>   Where we shall ere long climb together,
>   With you, my friend, with you.
>   Companion of the pitchy night,
>   When heavenward turns my face—
>   Thou art, indeed, my man."

With her woman companion she came to the mountainside. The sun was going down; they would have barely time to climb the ladder that was there and go into the cavern before the night fell. Then the ladder was taken away by witches who bore an enmity to Hi-i-aka; and the ghost body of Lo-hi-au wailed thinly and more faintly.

Hi-i-aka chanted an incantation that held the sun from sinking down. And while the sun stayed to give them light, she and her companion toiled up the cliff. They came to the entrance of the cave. Hi-i-aka caught in her hand Lo-hi-au's ghost body. They went within. Hi-i-aka directed her companion to take hold of the dead feet. The fluttering ghost body that she held in her hand she brought to the eye socket and strove to make it pass through at that place. With spells she strove to make the soul particle pass on. It went within; it reached the loins; it would pass no farther. Hi-i-aka forced it on. It went to the feet; the hands began to move, the eyelids quiver. Then breath came into the body. Hi-i-aka and her companion lifted it up and laid the body on a mat. With restoring herbs Hi-i-aka and her companion swathed the body from head to foot. But her companion said, "He will not recover in spite of all that you have done."

"I will make an incantation," Hi-i-aka said, "if it is rightly delivered, life will come back to him." Then she chanted:

> "Ho, comrades from the sacred plateau!
> Ho, comrades from the burning gulf!
> Hither fly with art and cunning:
> Ku, who fells and guides the war boat;
> Ku, who pilots us through dreamland;
> All ye gods of broad Hawaii;
> Kanaloa, guard well your tapus;
> Candle-maker, candle-snuffer;
> Goddess, too, of passions, visions;
> Lightning red all heaven filling—
> Pitchy darkness turned to brightness—
> Lono, come, thou God of Fire;
> Come, too, thou piercing eye of rain;
> Speed, speed, my prayer upon its quest!"

More and more incantations Hi-i-aka made as the night passed and the day following passed. The people of the place were kept at a dance so that Hi-i-aka's task might not be broken in on. She made her last and her mightiest incantation; the soul particle stayed in the body, and Prince Lo-hi-au lived again.

They brought him to the entrance of the cave. Three rainbows arched themselves from the mouth of the cave, and adown these three rainbows Prince Lo-hi-au, Hi-i-aka, and her companion went. To the beach they went. And in the ocean the three performed the cleansing rite. And now that the toil of the journey and the toil of restoring the man to life were past, Hi-i-aka thought upon the groves of lehua and upon her dear and lovely friend, Ho-po-e.

And now that the time had come for her to make the journey back she turned toward Hawaii and chanted:

> "Oh, care for my parks of lehua—
> How they bloom in the upland Ka-li'u!
> Long is my way and many a day
> Before you shall come to the bed of love,
> But, hark, the call of the lover,
> The voice of the lover, Lo-hi-au!"

And when they had passed across many of the islands, and had crossed their channels, and had come at last to Hawaii, Hi-i-aka sent her companion before her to let Pe-le know that Lo-hi-au was being brought to her. When she had come with Lo-hi-au to the eastern gate of the sun, when she had come to Puna, she went swiftly ahead of Prince Lo-hi-au that she might look over her own land.

Pe-le had broken out in her fires; in spite of the agreement she had made with her sister and her messenger, she had wasted with fire the lehua groves. No tree now stood decked with blossoms. And the life of Ho-po-e, Hi-i-aka's dear and lovely friend, was ended with her lehua groves.

Blackness and ruin were everywhere Hi-i-aka looked. She stood in a place that overlooked her well-loved land, and all the bitterness of her heart went into the chant that she made then:

> "On the heights of Poha-ke
> I stand, and look forth on Puna—
> Puna, pelted with bitter rain,
> Veiled with a downpour black as night!
> Gone, gone are my forests, lehuas
> Whose bloom once gave the birds nectar!
> Yet they were insured with a promise!"

Then she said, "I have faithfully kept the compact between

myself and my sister. I have not touched her lover, I have not let him caress me, I have not given him a kiss. Now that compact is at an end. I am free to treat this handsome man as my lover, this man who has had desire for me. And I will let Pe-le, with her own eyes, see the compact broken."

When he came to where she was, she took his hand; she made herself kind to him; she told him she had been longing for the time when her companion would have gone and they two would be together. Hand in hand they went over the blackened and wasted land. They came to where an unburnt lehua grew upon a rock. There Hi-i-aka gathered blossoms to make a wreath for Lo-hi-au.

And on the terrace of Ka-hoa-lii where they were in full view of Pe-le and her court, she had him sit beside her. She plaited wreaths of lehua blossoms for him. She put them around his neck, while he, knowing nothing of the eyes that were watching them, became ardent in love making.

"Draw nearer," said Hi-i-aka, "draw nearer, so that I may fasten this wreath around your neck." She put her arm around the neck of Lo-hi-au; her body inclined toward his. She drew him to herself. The sisters around Pe-le cried out at that. "Hi-i-aka kisses Lo-hi-au! Look, Hi-i-aka kisses Lo-hi-au." "Mouths were made for kissing," Pe-le said, but the flame came into her eyes.

III.

THEN Pe-le commanded her sisters to put on their robes of fire, and go forth and destroy Lo-hi-au. In their robes of fire they went to where he was; when they came to him they threw cinders upon his feet and went away again. But Pe-le knew that they had made only a pretence of destroying the man. The caldron within her pit bubbled up; she called upon her helpers, upon Lono-makua, Ku-pulupulu, Kumoku-halli, Ku-ala-na-wao. At first they would not help her to destroy Lo-hi-au; rather, with their own hands, did they roll the fires back into the pit. Then did Pe-le threaten her helpers; then did Lono-makua go forth to do her bidding.

Lo-hi-au saw the fires coming toward him, and he chanted:

> "All about is flame—the rock plain rent;
> The coco palms that tufted the plain
> Are gone, all gone, clean down to Ka-poho.
> On rushes the dragon with flaming mouth,
> Eating its way to Oma'o-lala.
> For tinder it has the hair of the fern.
> A ghastly rain blots out the sky;
> The sooty birds of storm whirl through the vault;
> Heaven groans, adrip, as with dragon blood!"

The fires that rolled toward them spared Hi-i-aka. Lo-hi-au, choked by the vapor, fell down, and the lava flow went over him.

So Hi-i-aka lost the one whom she had come to love, as she had lost her lehua groves and her dear and lovely friend, Ho-po-e, through the rage of her sister, the dread Goddess. And as for Pe-le, she would have broken up the strata of the earth, and would have let the sea rise up through and destroy the islands, if Ka-ne had not appeared before her—Ka-ne the Earth-Shaper. Ka-ne soothed her mind, and she went back to the Pit, and sat amongst her sisters.

Once a man who was a great sorcerer came down into the Pit. "What is the purpose of your visit?" he was asked.

"I have come to know why Lo-hi-au, my friend, has been destroyed," he said.

"He and Hi-i-aka kissed and the man was tapu for Pe-le," the sisters answered.

"He tasted death at Haena. Why was he made taste death again in Hawaii?"

Pe-le, seated at the back of the Pit, spoke: "What is it that you say? That Lo-hi-au tasted death at Haena?"

"Yes. Hi-i-aka brought his soul and his body together again. Then they sailed for Hawaii."

Then said Pe-le to her youngest sister: "Is this true? Is it true that you found Lo-hi-au dead and that you restored him to life?"

"It is true. And it is true that not until you had destroyed my friend Ho-po-e did I give a caress to Lo-hi-au."

So Hi-i-aka said, and Pe-le, the Woman of the Pit, became silent. Then the sorcerer, Lo-hi-au's friend, said, "I would speak to Pe-le. But which is Pe-le? I have a test. Let me hold the hand of each of you, O Divine Woman, so that I may know which of you is the Goddess."

He took the hand of each of Pe-le's sisters, and held the hand to his cheek. He held the hollow palm to his ear. Each hand that was given to him had only a natural warmth when it was put to his cheek. Then he took the hand of a hag whose skin was rugged and blackened, whose hair was the color of cinders, whose eyes were red. The hand was burning on his cheek. From the hollow of the hand came reverberations of the sounds made by fountains of fire. "This is Pe-le," said the man, and he bent down and adored her.

Then Pe-le, loving this man who was Lo-hi-au's friend, and knowing that Hi-i-aka had been faithful in her service to her, softened, and would have Lo-hi-au brought to life again. But only one who was in far Kahiki possessed the power to restore Lo-hi-au to life. This was Kane-milo-hai, Pe-le's brother.

And Kane-milo-hai, coming over the waters in his shell canoe, found Lo-hi-au's spirit, in the form of a bird, flitting over the waters. He took it, and he brought it to where Lo-hi-au lay. He broke up the lava in which the body was set, and he formed the body out of the fragments, restoring to it the lineaments that Lo-hi-au had. Then he brought the spirit back into the body.

And afterward it happened that Hi-i-aka, wandering where the lehua groves were growing again, and knowing that after dire destruction a new world had come into existence, heard the chant:

> "Puna's plain takes the color of scarlet—
> Red as heart's blood the bloom of lehua
> The nymphs of the Pit string hearts in a wreath:
> O the pangs of the Pit, Ki-lau-ea!"

Hi-i-aka went to where the chant came from; she discovered Lo-hi-au restored to life once more. With him she wandered through the land below Ki-lau-ea. Men and women were peopling the land, and the Goddess of the Pit was not now so terror-inspiring.

THE SEVEN
GREAT DEEDS
OF MA-UI

THERE is no hero who is more famous than Ma-ui. In all the islands of the Great Ocean, from Kahiki-mo-e to Hawaii nei, his name and his deeds are spoken of. His deeds were many, but seven of them were very great, and it is about those seven great deeds that I shall tell you.

How Ma-ui Won a Place for Himself in the House.

WHEN Ma-ui, the last of her five sons, was born, his mother thought she would have no food for him. So she took him down to the shore of the sea, she cut off her hair and tied it around him, and she gave him to the waves. But Ma-ui was not drowned in the sea: first of all the jellyfish came; it folded him in its softness, and it kept him warm while he floated on. And then the God of the Sea found the child and took charge of him: he brought him to his house and warmed and cherished him, and little Ma-ui grew up in the land where lived the God of the Sea.

But while he was still a boy he went back to his mother's country. He saw his mother and his four brothers, and he followed them into a house; it was a house that all the people of the country were going into. He sat there with his brothers. And when his mother called her children to take them home, she found this strange child with them. She did not know him, and she would not take him with the rest of the children. But Ma-ui followed them. And when his four brothers came out of their own house they found him there, and he played with them. At first they played hide-and-seek, but then they made themselves spears from canes and began throwing the spears at the house.

The slight spears did not go through the thatch of grass that

was at the outside of the house. And then Ma-ui made a charm
over the cane that was his spear—a charm that toughened it and
made it heavy. He flung it again, and a great hole was made in
the grass thatch of the house. His mother came out to chastise
the boy and drive him away. But when she stood at the door
and saw him standing there so angry, and saw how he was able
to break down the house with the throws of his spear, she knew
in him the great power that his father had, and she called to him
to come into the house. He would not come in until she had laid
her hands upon him. When she did this his brothers were jealous
that their mother made so much of this strange boy, and they
did not want to have him with them. It was then that the elder
brother spoke and said, "Never mind; let him be with us and
be our dear brother." And then they all asked him to come into
the house.

The doorposts, Short Post and Tall Post, that had been put
there to guard the house, would not let him come in. Then Ma-ui
lifted up his spear, and he threw it at Tall Post and overthrew
him. He threw his spear again and overthrew Short Post. And
after that he went into his mother's house and was with his
brothers. The overthrowing of the two posts that guarded the
house was the first of the great deeds of Ma-ui.

In those days, say the people who know the stories of the old
times, the birds were not seen by the men and women of the
Islands. They flew around the houses, and the flutter of their
wings was heard, and the stirring of the branches and the leaves
as they were lit upon. Then there would be music. But the people
who had never seen the birds thought that this was music made
by gods who wanted to remain unseen by the people. Ma-ui
could see the birds; he rejoiced in their brilliant colors, and
when he called to them they would come and rest upon the
branches around the place where he was; there they would sing
their happiest songs to him.

There was a visitor who came from another land to the

country that Ma-ui lived in. He boasted of all the wonderful things that were in his country, and it seemed to the people of Ma-ui's land that they had nothing that was fine or that could be spoken about. Then Ma-ui called to the birds. They came and they made music on every side. The visitor who had boasted so much was made to wonder, and he said that there was nothing in his country that was so marvelous as the music made by Ma-ui's friends, the birds.

Then, that they might be honored by all, Ma-ui said a charm by which the birds came to be seen by men—the red birds, the i-i-wi and the aha-hani, and the yellow birds, the o-o and the mamo, and all the other bright birds. The delight of seeing them was equal to the delight of hearing the music that they made. Ever afterward the birds were seen and heard, and the people all rejoiced in them. This Ma-ui did when he was still a boy growing up with his brothers and with his sister in his mother's house. But this is not counted amongst the great deeds of Ma-ui the hero.

How Ma-ui Lifted Up the Sky.

THEN he lifted up the sky to where it is now. This was the second of Ma-ui's great deeds.

When he was growing up in his mother's house the sky was so low that the trees touched it and had their leaves flattened out. Men and women burned with the heat because the sky was so near to them. The clouds were so close that there was much darkness on the earth. Something had to be done about it, and Ma-ui made up his mind that he would lift up the sky.

Somewhere he got a mark tattooed on his arm that was a magic mark and that gave him great strength. Then he went to lift up the sky. And from some woman he got a drink that made his strength greater. "Give me to drink out of your gourd," he said, "and I will push up the sky." The woman gave him her gourd to drink from. Then Ma-ui pushed at the sky. He lifted it high, to where the trees have their tops now. He pushed at it again, and he put it where the mountains have their tops now. And then he pushed it to where it rests, on the tops of the highest mountains.

Then the men and women were able to walk about all over the earth, and they had light now and clear air. The trees grew higher and higher, and they grew more and more fruit. But even to this day their leaves are flattened out: it is from the time when their leaves were flattened against the sky.

When the sky was lifted up Ma-ui went and made a kite for himself. From his mother he got the largest and strongest piece of tapa cloth she had ever made, and he formed it into a kite with a frame and cross-sticks of hau wood. The tail of the kite was fifteen fathoms long, and he got a line of olona vine for it that was twenty times forty fathoms in length. He started the kite. But it rose very slowly; the wind barely held it up.

Then the people said: "Look at Ma-ui! He lifted the sky up, and now he can't fly a kite." Ma-ui was made angry when he heard them say this: he drew the kite this way and that way, but still he was not able to make it rise up. He cried out his incantation—

"Strong wind, come;
Soft wind, come"—

but still the kite would not rise.

Then he remembered that in the Valley of Wai-pio there was a wizard who had control of the winds. Over the mountains and down into the valley Ma-ui went. He saw the calabash that the wizard kept the winds in, and he asked him to loose them and direct them to blow along the river to the place where he was going to fly his kite. Then Ma-ui went back. He stood with his feet upon the rocks along the bank of the Wai-lu-ku River; he stood there braced to hold his kite, and where he stood are the marks of his feet to this day. He called out:

"O winds, winds of Wai-pio,
   Come from the calabash—'the Calabash of Perpetual Winds.'
   O wind, O wind of Hilo,
   Come quickly; come with power."

The call that Ma-ui gave went across the mountains and down into the valley of Wai-pio. No sooner did he hear it than the wizard opened his calabash. The winds rushed out. They went into the bay of Hilo, and they dashed themselves against the water. The call of Ma-ui came to them:

"O winds, winds of Hilo,
   Hurry, hurry and come to me."

The winds turned from the sea. They rushed along the river. They came to where Ma-ui stood, and then they saw the great, strange bird that he held.

They wanted to fall upon that bird and dash it up against the sky. But the great kite was strong. The winds flung it up and flung it this way and that way. But they could not carry it off or dash it against the sky as they wanted to.

Ma-ui rejoiced. How grand it was to hold a kite that the winds strove to tear away! He called out again:

"O winds, O winds of Hilo,
   Come to the mountains, come."

Then came the west wind that had been dashing up waves in the bay of Hilo. It joined itself with the north wind and the east wind, the two winds that had been tearing and pushing at Ma-ui's kite. Now, although the kite was made of the strongest tapa, and although it had been strengthened in every cunning way that Ma-ui knew, it was flung here and flung there. Ma-ui let his line out; the kite was borne up and up and above the mountains. And now he cried out to the kite that he had made:

> "Climb up, climb up
> To the highest level of the heavens,
> To all the sides of the heavens.
> Climb thou to thy ancestor,
> To the sacred bird in the heavens."

The three winds joined together, and now they made a fiercer attack upon Ma-ui's kite. The winds tore and tossed it. Then the line broke in Ma-ui's hands.

The winds flung the kite across the mountains. And then, to punish it for having dared to face the heavens, they rammed it down into the volcano, and stirred up the fires against it.

Then Ma-ui made for himself another kite. He flew it, and rejoiced in the flying of it, and all who saw him wondered at how high his kite went and how gracefully it bore itself in the heavens. But never again did he call upon the great winds to help him in his sport. Sometimes he would fasten his line to the black stones in the bed of the Wai-lu-ku River, and he would let the kite soar upward and range here and there. He knew by watching his soaring kite whether it would be dry and pleasant weather, and he showed his neighbors how they might know it. "Eh, neighbor," one would say to another, "it is going to be dry weather; look how Ma-ui's kite keeps in the sky." They knew that they could go to the fields to work and spread out their tapa to dry, for as long as the kite soared the rain would not fall.

Ma-ui learned what a strong pull the fierce winds had. He used to bring his kite with him when he went out on the ocean in his canoe. He would let it free; then, fastening his line to the canoe, he would let the wind that pulled the kite pull him along. By flying his kite he learned how to go more swiftly over the ocean in his canoe, and how to make further voyages than ever a man made before.

Nevertheless, his kite flying is not counted amongst the great deeds of Ma-ui.

How Ma-ui Fished Up the Great Island.

Now, although Ma-ui had done deeds as great as these, he was not thought so very much of in his own house. His brothers complained that when he went fishing with them he caught no fish, or, if he drew one up, it was a fish that had been taken on a hook belonging to one of them and that Ma-ui had managed to get tangled on to his own line. And yet Ma-ui had invented many things that his brothers made use of. At first they had spears with smooth heads on them: if they struck a bird, the bird was often able to flutter away, drawing away from the spearhead that had pierced a wing. And if they struck through a fish, the fish was often able to wriggle away. Then Ma-ui put barbs upon his spear, and his spearhead held the birds and the fish. His brothers copied the spearhead that he made, and after that they were able to kill and secure more birds and fish than ever before.

He made many things that they copied, and yet his brothers thought him a lazy and a shiftless fellow, and they made their mother think the same about him. They were the better fishermen—that was true; indeed, if there were no one but Ma-ui to go fishing, Hina-of-the-Fire, his mother, and Hina-of-the-Sea, his sister, would often go hungry.

At last Ma-ui made up his mind to do some wonderful fishing; he might not be able to catch the fine fish that his brothers desired—the u-lua and the pi-mo-e—but he would take up something from the bottom of the sea that would make his brothers forget that he was the lazy and the shiftless one.

He had to make many plans and go on many adventures before he was ready for this great fishing. First he had to get a fishhook that was different from any fishhook that had ever been in the world before. In those days fishhooks were made out of bones—there was nothing else to make fishhooks out of

—and Ma-ui would have to get a wonderful bone to form into a hook. He went down into the underworld to get that bone.

He went to where his ancestress was. On one side she was dead and on the other side she was a living woman. From the side of her that was dead Ma-ui took a bone—her jawbone—and out of this bone he made his fishhook. There was never a fishhook like it in the world before, and it was called "Ma-nai-i-ka-lani," meaning "made fast to the heavens." He told no one about the wonderful fishhook he had made for himself.

He had to get a different bait from any bait that had ever been used in the world before. His mother had sacred birds, the alae, and he asked her to give him one of them for bait. She gave him one of her birds.

Then Ma-ui, with his bait and his hook hidden, and with a line that he had made from the strongest olona vines, went down to his brothers' canoe. "Here is Ma-ui," they said when they saw him, "here is Ma-ui, the lazy and the shiftless, and we have sworn that we will never let him come again with us in our canoe." They pushed out when they saw him coming; they paddled away, although he begged them to take him with them.

He waited on the beach. His brothers came back, and they had to tell him that they had caught no fish. Then he begged them to go back to sea again and to let him go this time in their canoe. They let him in, and they paddled off. "Farther and farther out, my brothers," said Ma-ui; "out there is where the u-lua and the pi-mo-e are." They paddled far out. They let down their lines, but they caught no fish. "Where are the u-lua and the pi-mo-e that you spoke of?" said his brothers to him. Still he told them to go farther and farther out. At last they got tired with paddling, and they wanted to go back.

Then Ma-ui put a sail upon the canoe. Farther and farther out into the ocean they went. One of the brothers let down a line, and a great fish drew on it. They pulled. But what came out of the depths was a shark. They cut the line and let the shark away. The brothers were very tired now. "Oh, Ma-ui," they said, "as ever, thou art lazy and shiftless. Thou hast brought us out all this way, and thou wilt do nothing to help us. Thou hast let down no line in all the sea we have crossed."

It was then that Ma-ui let down his line with the magic hook upon it, the hook that was baited with the struggling alae bird. Down, down went the hook that was named "Ma-nai-i-ka-lani." Down through the waters the hook and the bait went. Ka-uni ho-kahi, Old One Tooth, who holds fast the land to the bottom of the sea, was there. When the sacred bird came near him he took it in his mouth. And the magic hook that Ma-ui had made held fast in his jaws.

Ma-ui felt the pull upon the line. He fastened the line to the canoe, and he bade his brothers paddle their hardest, for now the great fish was caught. He dipped his own paddle into the sea, and he made the canoe dash on.

The brothers felt a great weight grow behind the canoe. But still they paddled on and on. Weighty and more weighty became the catch; harder and harder it became to pull it along. As they struggled on Ma-ui chanted a magic chant, and the weight came with them.

> "O Island, O great Island,
> O Island, O great Island!
> Why art thou
> Sulkily biting, biting below?
> Beneath the earth
> The power is felt,
> The foam is seen:
> Come,
> O thou loved grandchild
> Of Kanaloa."

On and on the canoe went, and heavier and heavier grew

what was behind them. At last one of the brothers looked back. At what he saw he screamed out in affright. For there, rising behind them, a whole land was rising up, with mountains upon it. The brother dropped his paddle when he saw what had been fished up; as he dropped his paddle the line that was fastened to the jaws of old Ka-uni ho-kahi broke.

What Ma-ui fished up would have been a mainland, only that his brother's paddle dropped and the line broke. Then only an island came up out of the water. If more land had come up, all the islands that we know would have been joined in one.

There are people who say that his sister, Hina-of-the-Sea, was near at the time of that great fishing. They say she came floating out on a calabash. When Ma-ui let down the magic hook with their mother's sacred bird upon it, Hina-of-the-Sea dived down and put the hook into the mouth of Old One Tooth, and then pulled at the line to let Ma-ui know that the hook was in his jaws. Some people say this, and it may be the truth. But whether or not, everyone, on every island in the Great Ocean, from Kahiki-mo-e to Hawaii nei, knows that Ma-ui fished up a great island for men to live on. And this fishing was the third of Ma-ui's great deeds.

How Ma-ui Snared the Sun and Made Him Go More Slowly Across the Heavens.

THE Sky had been lifted up, and another great island had come from the grip of Old One Tooth and was above the waters. The world was better now for men and women to live in. But still there were miseries in it, and the greatest of these miseries was on account of the heedlessness of the Sun.

For the Sun in those days made his way too quickly across the world. He hurried so that little of his heat got to the plants and the fruits, and it took years and years for them to ripen. The farmers working on their patches would not have time in the

light of a day to put down their crop into the ground, so quickly
the Sun would rush across the heavens, and the fishermen would
barely have time to launch their canoes and get to the fishing
grounds when the darkness would come on. And the women's
tasks were never finished. It was theirs to make the tapa cloth: a
woman would begin at one end of the board to beat the bark
with her four-sided mallet, and she would be only at the middle
of the board by the time the sunset came. When she was ready
to go on with the work next day, the Sun would be already halfway across the heavens.

Ma-ui, when he was a child, used to watch his mother making
tapa, and as he grew up he pitied her more and more because of
all the toil and trouble that she had. She would break the
branches from the ma-ma-ka trees and from the wau-ka trees
and soak them in water until their bark was easily taken off.
Then she would take off the outer bark, leaving the inner bark
to be worked upon. She would take the bundles of the wet inner
bark and lay them on the tapa board and begin pounding them
with little clubs. And then she would use her four-sided mallet
and beat all the soft stuff into little thin sheets. Then she would
paste the little sheets together, making large cloths. This was
tapa—the tapa that it was every woman's business in those days
to make. As soon as morning reddened the clouds Ma-ui's
mother, Hina-of-the-Fire, would begin her task: she would
begin beating the softened bark at one end of the board, and she
would be only in the middle of the board when the sunset came.
And when she managed to get the tapa made she could never get
it dried in a single day, so quickly the Sun made his way across
the heavens. Ma-ui pitied his mother because of her unceasing
toil.

He greatly blamed the Sun for his inconsiderateness of the
people of the world. He took to watching the Sun. He began to
know the path by which the Sun came over the great mountain
Ha-le-a-ka-la (but in those days it was not called Ha-le-a-ka-la,

the House of the Sun, but A-hele-a-ka-la, the Rays of the Sun). Through a great chasm in the side of this mountain the Sun used to come.

He told his mother that he was going to do something to make the Sun have more considerateness for the men and women of the world. "You will not be able to make him do anything about it," she said; "the Sun always went swiftly, and he will always go swiftly." But Ma-ui said that he would find a way to make the Sun remember that there were people in the world and that they were not at all pleased with the way he was going on.

Then his mother said: "If you are going to force the Sun to go more slowly you must prepare yourself for a great battle, for the Sun is a great creature, and he has much energy. Go to your grandmother who lives on the side of Ha-le-a-ka-la," said she (but it was called A-hele-a-ka-la then), "and beg her to give you her counsel, and also to give you a weapon to battle with the Sun."

So Ma-ui went to his grandmother who lived on the side of the great mountain. Ma-ui's grandmother was the one who cooked the bananas that the Sun ate as he came through the great chasm in the mountain. "You must go to the place where there is a large wili-wili tree growing," said his mother. "There the Sun stops to eat the bananas that your grandmother cooks for him. Stay until the rooster that watches beside the wili-wili tree crows three times. Your grandmother will come out then with a bunch of bananas. When she lays them down, do you take them up. She will bring another bunch out, and do you take that up too. When all her bananas are gone she will search for the one who took them. Then do you show yourself to her. Tell her that you are Ma-ui and that you belong to Hina-of-the-Fire."

So Ma-ui went up the side of the mountain that is now called Ha-le-a-ka-la, but that then was called A-hele-a-ka-la, the Rays of the Sun. He came to where a great wili-wili tree was growing.

There he waited. The rooster crew three times, and then an old woman came out with a bunch of bananas. He knew that this was his grandmother. She laid the bananas down to cook them, and as she did so Ma-ui snatched them away. When she went to pick up the bunch she cried out, "Where are the bananas that I have to cook for my lord, the Sun?" She went within and got another bunch, and this one, too, Ma-ui snatched away. This he did until the last bunch of bananas that his grandmother had was taken.

She was nearly blind, so she could not find him with her eyes. She sniffed around, and at last she got the smell of a man. "Who are you?" she said. "I am Ma-ui, and I belong to Hina-of-the-Fire," said he. "What have you come for?" asked his grandmother. "I have come to chastise the Sun and to make him go more slowly across the heavens. He goes so fast now that my mother cannot dry the tapa that she takes all the days of the year to beat out."

The old woman considered all that Ma-ui said to her. She knew that he was a hero born, because the birds sang, the pebbles rumbled, the grass withered, the smoke hung low, the rainbow appeared, the thunder was heard, the hairless dogs were seen, and even the ants in the grass were heard to sing in his praise. She decided to give help to him. And she told him what preparations he was to make for his battle with the Sun.

First of all he was to get sixteen of the strongest ropes that ever were made. So as to be sure they were the strongest, he was to knit them himself. And he was to make nooses for them out of the hair of the head of his sister, Hina-of-the-Sea. When the ropes were ready he was to come back to her, and she would show him what else he had to do.

Ma-ui made the sixteen ropes; he made them out of the strongest fiber, and his sister, Hina-of-the-Sea, gave him the hair of her head to make into nooses. Then, with the ropes and the nooses upon them, Ma-ui went back to his grandmother. She told him where to set the nooses, and she gave him a magic stone ax with which to do battle with the Sun.

He set the nooses as snares for the Sun, and he dug a hole beside the roots of the wili-wili tree, and in that hole he hid himself. Soon the first ray of light, the first leg of the Sun, came over the mountain wall. It was caught in one of the nooses that Ma-ui had set. One by one the legs of the Sun came over the rim, and one by one they were caught in the nooses. One leg was left hanging down the side of the mountain: it was hard for the Sun to move that leg. At last this last leg came slowly over the edge of the mountain and was caught in the snare. Then Ma-ui gathered up the ropes and tied them to the great wili-wili tree.

When the Sun saw that his sixteen legs were held fast by the nooses that Ma-ui had set he tried to back down the mountain-side and into the sea again. But the ropes held him, and the wili-wili tree stood the drag of the ropes. The Sun could not get away. Then he turned all his burning strength upon Ma-ui. They fought. The man began to strike at the Sun with his magic ax of stone; and never before did the Sun get such a beating. "Give me my life," said the Sun. "I will give you your life," said Ma-ui, "if you promise to go slowly across the heavens." At last the Sun promised to do what Ma-ui asked him.

They entered into an agreement with each other, Ma-ui and the Sun. There should be longer days, the Sun making his course slower. But every six months, in the winter, the Sun might go as fast as he had been in the habit of going. Then Ma-ui let the Sun out of the snares which he had set for him. But, lest he should ever forget the agreement he had made and take to traveling swiftly again, Ma-ui left all the ropes and the nooses on the side of Ha-le-a-ka-la, so that he might see them every day that he came across the rim of the mountain. And the mountain was not called A-hele-a-ka-la, the Rays of the Sun, any more, but Ha-le-a-ka-la, the House of the Sun. After that came the saying of the people, "Long shall be the daily journey of the Sun, and he shall give light for all the peoples' toil." And Ma-ui's mother, Hina-of-the-Fire, learned that she could pound on the tapa board until she was tired, and the farmers could plant and take care of their crops, and the fishermen could go out to the deep sea and fish and come back, and the fruits and the plants got heat enough to make them ripen in their season.

How Ma-ui Won Fire for Men.

Ma-ui's mother must have known about fire and the use of fire; else why should she have been called Hina-of-the-Fire, and how did it come that her birds, the alae, knew where fire was hidden and how to make it blaze up? Hina must have known about fire. But her son had to search and search for fire. The people who lived in houses on the Islands did not know of it: they had to eat raw roots and raw fish, and they had to suffer the cold. It was for them that Ma-ui wanted to get fire; it was for them that he went down to the lower world, and that he went searching through the upper world for it.

In Kahiki-mo-e they have a tale about Ma-ui that the Hawaiians do not know. There they tell how he went down to the lower world and sought out his great-great-grandmother, Ma-hui'a. She was glad to see Ma-ui, of whom she had heard in the lower world; and when he asked her to give him fire to take to the upper world, she plucked a nail off her finger and gave it to him.

In this nail, fire burned. Ma-ui went to the upper world with it. But in crossing a stream of water he let the nail drop into it. And so he lost the fire that his great-great-grandmother had given him.

He went back to her again. And again Ma-hui'a plucked off a fingernail and gave it to him. But when he went to the upper world and went to cross the stream, he let this burning nail also drop into the water. Again he went back, and his great-great-grandmother plucked off a third nail for him. And this went on, Ma-ui letting the nails fall into the water, and Ma-hui'a giving him the nails off her fingers, until at last all the nails of all her fingers were given to him.

But still he went on letting the burning nails fall into the water that he had to cross, and at last the nails of his great-great-grandmother's toes as well as the nails of her fingers were given to him—all but the nail on the last of her toes. Ma-ui went back to her to get this last nail. Then Ma-hui'a became blazing angry; she plucked the nail off, but instead of giving it to him she flung it upon the ground.

Fire poured out of the nail and took hold on everything. Ma-ui ran to the upper world, and Ma-hui'a in her anger ran after him. He dashed into the water. But now the forests were blazing, and the earth was burning, and the water was boiling. Ma-ui ran on, and Ma-hui'a ran behind him. As he ran he chanted a magic incantation for rain to come, so that the burning might be put out:

> "To the roaring thunder;
> To the great rain—the long rain;
> To the drizzling rain—the small rain;
> To the rain pattering on the leaves.
> These are the storms, the storms
> Cause them to fall;
> To pour in torrents."

The rain came on—the long rain, the small rain, the rain that patters on the leaves; storms came, and rain in torrents. The fire that raged in the forests and burned on the ground was drowned out. And Ma-hui'a, who had followed him, was nearly drowned by the torrents of rain. She saw her fire, all the fire that was in the lower and in the upper worlds, being quenched by the rain.

She gathered up what fragments of fire she could, and she hid them in barks of different trees so that the rain could not get at them and quench them. Ma-ui's mother must have known where his great-great-grandmother hid the fire. If she did not, her sacred birds, the alae, knew it. They were able to take the barks of the trees and, by rubbing them together, to bring out fire.

In Hawaii they tell how Ma-ui and his brothers used to go out fishing every day, and how, as soon as they got far out to sea, they would see smoke rising on the mountainside. "Behold," they would say, "there is a fire. Whose can it be?" "Let us hasten to the shore and cook our fish at that fire," another would say.

So, with the fish that they had caught, Ma-ui and his brothers would hasten to the shore. The swiftest of them would run up the mountainside. But when he would get to where the smoke had been, all he would see would be the alae scratching clay over burnt-out sticks. The alae would leave the place where they had been seen, and Ma-ui would follow them from place to place, hoping to catch them while their fire was lighted.

He would send his brothers off fishing, and he himself would watch for the smoke from the fire that the alae would kindle. But they would kindle no fire on the days that he did not go out in the canoe with his brothers. "We cannot have our cooked bananas today," the old bird would say to the young birds, "for the swift son of Hina is somewhere near, and he would come upon us before we put out our fire. And remember that the guardian of the fire told us never to show a man where it is hidden or how it is taken out of its hiding place."

Then Ma-ui understood that the birds watched for his going and that they made no fire until they saw him out at sea in his canoe. He knew that they counted the men that went out, and that if he was not in the number they did no cooking that day. Every time he went in the canoe he saw smoke rising on the mountainside.

Then Ma-ui thought of a trick to play on them—on the

stingy alae that would not give fire, but left men to eat raw roots and raw fish. He rolled up a piece of tapa, and he put it into the canoe, making it like a man. Then he hid near the shore. The brothers went fishing, and the birds counted the figures in the canoe. "The swift son of Hina has gone fishing: we can have cooked bananas today." "Make the fire, make the fire, until we cook our bananas," said the young alae.

So they gathered the wood together, and they rubbed the barks, and they made the fire. The smoke rose up from it, and swift Ma-ui ran up the mountainside. He came upon the flock óf birds just as the old one was dashing water upon the embers. He caught her by the neck and held her.

"I will kill you," he said, "for hiding fire from men."

"If you kill me," said the old alae, "there will be no one to show you how to get fire."

"Show me how to get fire," said Ma-ui, "and I will let you go."

The cunning alae tried to deceive Ma-ui. She thought she would get him off his guard, that he would let go of her, and that she could fly away. "Go to the reeds and rub them together, and you will get fire," she said.

Ma-ui went to the reeds and rubbed them together. But still he held the bird by the neck. Nothing came out of the reeds but moisture. He squeezed her neck. "If you kill me, there will be no one to tell you where to get fire," said the cunning bird, still hoping to get him off his guard. "Go to the taro leaves and rub them together, and you will get fire."

Ma-ui held to the bird's neck. He went to the taro leaves and rubbed them together, but no fire came. He squeezed her neck harder. The bird was nearly dead now. But still she tried to deceive the man. "Go to the banana stumps and rub them together, and you will get fire," she said.

He went to the banana stumps and rubbed them together. But still no fire came. Then he gave the bird a squeeze that brought her near her death. She showed him then the trees to go to—the hau tree and the sandalwood tree. He took the barks of the trees and rubbed them, and they gave fire. And the sweet-smelling sandalwood he called "ili-aha"—that is, "fire bark"—because fire came most easily from the bark of that tree. With sticks from these trees Ma-ui went to men. He showed them how to get fire by rubbing them together. And never afterward had men to eat fish raw and roots raw. They could always have fire now.

The first stick he lighted he rubbed on the head of the bird that showed him at last where the fire was hidden. And that is the reason why the alae, the mud hen, has a red streak on her head to this day.

How Ma-ui Overcame Kuna Loa the Long Eel.

HINA-OF-THE-FIRE lived in a cave that the waters of the river streamed over, a cave that always had a beautiful rainbow glimmering across it. While her sons were away no enemy could come to Hina in this cave, for the walls of it went up straight and smooth. And there at the opening of the cave she used to sit, beating out her tapa in the long days that came after Ma-ui had snared the Sun and had made him go more slowly across the heavens.

In the river below there was one who was an enemy to Hina. This was Kuna Loa, the Long Eel. Once Kuna Loa had seen Hina on the bank of the river, and he had wanted her to leave her cave and come to his abode. But Hina-of-the-Fire would not go near the Long Eel. Then he had gone to her, and he had lashed her with his tail, covering her with the slime of the river. She told about the insults he had given her, and Ma-ui drove the Long Eel up the river, where he took shelter in the deep pools. Ma-ui broke down the banks of the deep pools with thrusts of his spear, but Kuna Loa, the Long Eel, was still able to escape from him. Now Ma-ui had gone away, and his mother,

Hina-of-the-Fire, kept within the cave, the smooth rock of which Kuna Loa could not climb.

The Long Eel came down the river. He saw Hina sitting in the mouth of the cave that had the rainbow glimmering across it, and he was filled with rage and a wish to destroy her. He took a great rock and he put it across the stream, filling it from bank to bank. Then he lashed about in the water in his delight at the thought of what was going to happen to Hina.

She heard a deeper sound in the water than she had ever heard before as she sat there. She looked down and she saw that the water was nearer to the mouth of the cave than she had ever seen it before. Higher and higher it came. And then Hina heard the voice of Kuna Loa rejoicing at the destruction that was coming to her. He raised himself up in the water and cried out to her: "Now your mighty son cannot help you. I will drown you with the waters of the river before he comes back to you, Hina."

And Hina-of-the-Fire cried, "Alas, alas," as she watched the waters mount up and up, for she knew that Ma-ui and her other sons were far away, and that there was none to help her against Kuna Loa, the Long Eel. But, even as she lamented, something was happening to aid Hina. For Ma-ui had placed above her cave a cloud that served her—"Ao-opua," "The Warning Cloud." Over the cave it rose now, giving itself a strange shape: Ma-ui would see it and be sure to know by its sign that something dire was happening in his mother's cave.

He was then on the mountain Ha-le-a-ka-la, the House of the Sun. He saw the strangely shaped cloud hanging over her cave, and he knew that some danger threatened his mother, Hina-of-the-Fire. He dashed down the side of the mountain, bringing with him the magic ax that his grandmother had given him for his battle with the Sun. He sprang into his canoe. With two strokes of his paddle he crossed the channel and was at the mouth of the Wai-lu-ku River. The bed of the river was empty of water, and Ma-ui left his canoe on the stones and went up toward Hina's cave.

The water had mounted up and up and had gone into the cave, and was spilling over Hina's tapa board. She was lamenting, and her heart was broken with the thought that neither Ma-ui nor his brothers would come until the river had drowned her in her cave.

Ma-ui was then coming up the bed of the river. He saw the great stone across the stream, and he heard Kuna Loa rejoicing over the destruction that was coming to Hina in her cave. With one stroke of his ax he broke the rock across. The water came through the break. He struck the rocks and smashed them. The river flowed down once more, and Hina was safe in her cave.

Kuna Loa heard the crash of the ax on the rock, and he knew that Ma-ui had come. He dashed up the stream to hide himself again in the deep pools. Ma-ui showed his mother that she was safe, and then he went following the Long Eel.

Kuna Loa had gone into a deep pool. Ma-ui flung burning stones into the water of that pool, making it boil up. Then Kuna Loa dashed into another pool. From pool to pool Ma-ui chased him, making the pools boil around him. (And there they boil to this day, although Kuna Loa is no longer there.) At last the Eel found a cave in the bottom of one of the pools, and he went and hid in it, and Ma-ui could not find him there, nor could the hot stones that Ma-ui threw into the water, making it boil, drive Kuna Loa out.

Hina thought she was safe from the Long Eel after that. She thought that his skin was so scalded by the boiling water that he had died in his cave. Down the river bank for water she would go, and sometimes she would stand on the bank all wreathed in flowers.

But one day, as she was standing on the bank of the river, Kuna Loa suddenly came up. Hina fled before him. The Eel was between her and her cave, and she could not get back to her shelter. She fled through the woods. And as she fled she shrieked out chants to Ma-ui: her chants went through the woods, and along the side of the mountain, and across the sea; they came at last up the side of Ha-le-a-ka-la, where her son Ma-ui was.

There were many people in the places that Hina fled through, but they could do nothing to help her against the Long Eel. He came swiftly after her. The people in the villages that they went through stood and watched the woman and the Eel that pursued her.

Where would she go now? The Long Eel was close behind her. Then Hina saw a breadfruit tree with great branches, and she climbed into it. Kuna Loa wound himself around the tree and came after her. But the branch that Hina was in was lifted up and up by the tree, and the Long Eel could not come to her.

And then Ma-ui came. He had dashed down the side of the mountain and had crossed the channel with two strokes of his paddles and had hurried along the track made by the Long Eel. Now he saw his mother in the branch that kept mounting up, and he saw Kuna Loa winding himself up after her. Ma-ui went into the tree. He struck the Eel a terrible blow and brought him to the ground. Then he sprang down and cut his head off. With other blows of his ax he cut the Eel all to pieces. He flung the head and the tail of Kuna Loa into the sea. The head turned into fish of many kinds, and the tail became the large conger eel of the sea. Other parts of the body turned into sea monsters of different kinds. And the blood of Kuna Loa, as it fell into the fresh water, became the common eels. The fresh and the salt water eels came into the world in this way, and Ma-ui, by killing the Long Eel, wrought the sixth of his great deeds.

The Search That Ma-ui's Brother Made for His Sister Hina-of-the-Sea.

Ma-ui had four brothers, and each of them was named Ma-ui. The doer of the great deeds was known as "the skilful Ma-ui," and the other four brothers were called "the forgetful Ma-uis."

But there was one brother who should not have been called "forgetful." He was the eldest brother, Ma-ui Mua, and he was sometimes called Lu-pe. He may have been forgetful about many things that the skilful Ma-ui took account of, but he was not forgetful of his sister, Hina-of-the-Sea.

His great and skilful brother had set Hina-of-the-Sea wandering. She was married, and her husband often went on journeys with the skilful Ma-ui. And once Ma-ui became angry with him because he ate the bait that they had taken with them for fishing; he became angry with his sister's husband, and in his anger he uttered a spell over him, and changed his form into the form of a dog.

When Hina-of-the-Sea knew that her husband was lost to her she went down to the shore and she chanted her own death song:

> "I weep, I call upon the steep billows of the sea,
>   And on him, the great, the ocean god;
>   The monsters, all now hidden,
>   To come and bury me,
>   Who am now wrapped in mourning.
>   Let the waves wear their mourning, too,
>   And sleep as sleeps the dead."

And after she had chanted this, she threw herself into the sea.

But the waves did not drown her. They carried her to a far land. There were no people there; according to the ancient chant—

> "The houses of Lima Loa stand,
>   But there are no people;
>   They are at Mana."

The people were by the sea, and two who were fishermen found her. They carried her to their hut, and when they had taken the sea weed and the sea moss from her body they saw what a beautiful woman she was. They brought her to their chief, and the chief took Hina-of-the-Sea for his wife.

But after a while he became forgetful of her. After another while he abused her. She had a child now, but she was very lonely, for she was in a far and a strange land.

> "The houses of Lima Loa stand,
>   But there are no people;
>   They are at Mana."

She was not forgotten, for Ma-ui Mua, her eldest brother, thought of her. In Kahiki-mo-e they tell of his search for her, and they say that when he heard of her casting herself into the sea, he took to his canoe and went searching all over the sea for her. He found new islands, islands that no one had ever been on before, and he went from island to island, ever hoping to find Hina-of-the-Sea. Far, far he went, and he found neither his sister nor anyone who knew about her.

> "The houses of Lima Loa stand,
>   But there are no people;
>   They are at Mana."

And every day Hina-of-the-Sea would go down to the shore of the land she was on, and she would call on her eldest brother:

> "O Lu-pe! Come over!
>   Take me and my child!"

Now one day, as Hina cried out on the beach, there came a canoe toward her. There was a man in the canoe; but Hina, hardly noticing him, still cried to the waves and the winds:

> "O Lu-pe! Come over!
>   Take me and my child!"

The man came up on the beach. He was worn with much travel, and he was white and old looking. He heard the cry that was sent to the waves and the winds, and he cried back in answer:

> "It is Lu-pe, yes, Lu-pe,
> The eldest brother;
> And I am here."

He knew Hina-of-the-Sea. He took her and her child in his canoe, rejoicing that his long search was over at last and that he had a sister again. He took her and her child to one of the islands which he had discovered.

And there Hina-of-the-Sea lived happily with her eldest brother, Ma-ui Mua, and there her child grew up to manhood. The story of her eldest brother's search for Hina is not told in Hawaii nei, and one has to go to Kahiki-mo-e to hear it. But in Hawaii nei they tell of a beautiful land that Ma-ui the Skilful came to in search of someone. It is the land, perhaps, that his brother and sister lived in—the beautiful land that is called Moana-liha-i-ka-wao-ke-le.

How Ma-ui Strove to Win Immortality for Men.

WOULD you hear the seventh and last of great Ma-ui's deeds? They do not tell of this deed in Hawaii nei, but they tell of it in Kahiki-mo-e. The last was the greatest of all Ma-ui's deeds, for it was his dangerous labor then to win the greatest boon for men—the boon of everlasting life.

He heard of the Goblin-Goddess who is called Hina-nui-ke-po, Great Hina-of-the-Night. It is she who brings death on all creatures. But if one could take the heart out of her body and give it to all the creatures of the earth to eat, they would live forever, and death would be no more in the world.

They tell how the Moon bathes in the Waters of Life, and

comes back to the world with her life renewed. And once Ma-ui caught and held the Moon. He said to her, "Let Death be short, and as you return with new strength let it be that men shall come back from Death with new strength." But the Moon said to Ma-ui, "Rather let Death be long, so that men may sigh and have sorrow. When a man dies, let him go into darkness and become as earth, so that those whom he leaves behind may weep and mourn for him." But for all that the Moon said to Ma-ui, he would not have it that men should go into the darkness forever and become as earth. The Moon showed him where Hina-of-the-Night had her abode. He looked over to her Island and saw her. Her eyes shone through the distance; he saw her great teeth that were like volcanic glass and her mouth that was wide like the mouth of a fish; he saw her hair that floated all around her like seaweed in the sea.

He saw her and was afraid; even great Ma-ui was made afraid by the Goblin-Goddess, Great Hina-of-the-Night. But he remembered that he had said that he would find a way of giving everlasting life to men and to all creatures, and he thought and thought of how he could come to the Goblin-Goddess and take the heart out of her body.

It was his task then to draw all creatures to him and to have them promise him that they would help him against the Goblin-Goddess. And when at last he was ready to go against her the birds went with him. He came to the island where she was, Great Hina-of-the-Night. She was sleeping, and all her guards were around her. Ma-ui passed through her guards. He prepared to enter her terrible open mouth, and bring back her heart to give to all the creatures of the earth.

And at last he stood ready to go between the jaws that had the fearful teeth that were sharp like volcanic glass. He stood there in the light of a sun-setting, his body tall and fine and tattooed all over with the histories of his great deeds. He stood there, and then he gave warning to all the birds that none of them was to sing or to laugh until he was outside her jaws again with the heart of the Goblin-Goddess in his hands.

He went within the jaws of Great Hina-of-the-Night. He passed the fearful teeth that were sharp like volcanic glass. He went down into her stomach. And then he seized upon her heart. He came back again as far as her jaws, and he saw the sky beyond them.

Then a bird sang or a bird laughed—either the e-le-pa-io sang, or the water wagtail laughed—and the Goblin-Goddess wakened up. She caught Ma-ui in her great teeth, and she tore him across. There was darkness then, and the crying of all the birds.

Thus died Ma-ui who raised the sky and who fished up the land, who made the Sun go more slowly across the heavens, and who brought fire to men. Thus died Ma-ui, with the Meat of Immortality in his hands. And since his death no one has ever ventured near the lair of Hina-nui-ke-po, the Goblin-Goddess.

THE
ME-NE-HU-NE

K A-U-KI-U-KI—that was the name of the Me-ne-hu-ne
who boasted to the rest of his folk that he could catch
the Moon by holding on to her legs; Ka-u-ki-u-ki, the
Angry One.

The Me-ne-hu-ne folk worked only at night; and if one could
catch and hold on to the legs of the Moon, the night would not
go so quickly, and more work could be done by them. They were
all very great workers. But when the Angry One made his boast
about catching the legs of the Moon, the rest of the Me-ne-
hu-ne made mock of him. That made Ka-u-ki-u-ki more angry
still. Straightway he went up to the top of the highest hill. He
sat down to rest himself after his climb; then, they say, the Owl
of Ka-ne came and sat on the stones and stared at him. Ka-u-
ki-u-ki might well have been frightened, for the big, round-eyed
bird could easily have flown away with him, or flown away with
any of the Me-ne-hu-ne folk. For they were all little men, and
none of them was higher than the legs of one of us—no, not

even their Kings and Chiefs. Little men, broad-shouldered and sturdy and very active—such were the Me-ne-hu-ne in the old days, and such are the Me-ne-hu-ne today.

But Ka-u-ki-u-ki was brave: the Me-ne-hu-ne stared back at the Owl, and the Owl of Ka-ne stared back at the little man, and at last the bird flew away. Then it was too late for him to try to lay hold on the legs of the Moon that night.

That was a long time ago, when the Me-ne-hu-ne were very many in our land. They lived then in the Valley of Lani-hula. There they planted taro in plants that still grow there—plants that they brought back with them from Kahiki-mo-e after they had been there. It was they who planted the breadfruit tree first in that valley.

Our fathers say that when the men folk of the Me-ne-hu-ne stood together in those days they could form two rows reaching all the way from Maka-weli to Wai-lua. And with their women and children there were so many of them that the only fish of which each of the Me-ne-hu-ne could have one was the shrimp, the littlest and the most plentiful fish in our waters.

For the rest of their food they had *hau-pia*, a pudding made of arrowroot sweetened with the milk of coconut; they had squash and they had sweet potato pudding. They ate fern fronds and the cooked young leaves of the taro. They had carved wooden dishes for their food. For their games they had spinning tops which they made out of ku-kui nuts, and they played at casting the arrow, a game which they called *Kea-pua*. They had boxing and wrestling, too, and they had tug-of-war: when one team was about to be beaten all the others jumped in and helped them. They had sled races; they would race their sleds down the steep sides of hills; if the course were not slippery already, they would cover it with rushes so that the sleds could go more easily and more swiftly.

But their great sport was to jump off the cliffs into the sea. They would throw a stone off the cliff and dive after it and touch the bottom as it touched the bottom. Once, when some of them were bathing, a shark nearly caught one of the Me-ne-hu-ne. A-a-ka was his name. Then they all swam ashore, and they made plans for punishing the shark that had treated them so. Their wise men told them what to do. They were to gather the morning-glory vine and make a great basket with it. Then they were to fill the basket with bait and lower it into the sea. Always the Me-ne-hu-ne worked together; they worked together very heartily when they went to punish the shark.

They made the basket; they filled it with bait, and they lowered it into the sea. The shark got into the basket, and the Me-ne-hu-ne caught him. They pulled him within the reef, and they left him there in the shallow water until the birds came and ate him up.

One of them caught a large fish there. The fish tried to escape, but the little man held bravely to him. The fish bit him and lashed him with its tail and drew blood from the Me-ne-hu-ne. The place where his blood poured out is called Ka-a-le-le to this day—for that was the name of the Me-ne-hu-ne who struggled with the fish.

Once they hollowed out a great stone and they gave it to their head fisherman for a house. He would sit in his hollow stone all day and fish for his people.

No cliff was too steep for them to climb; indeed, it was they who planted the wild taro on the cliffs; they planted it in the swamps too, and on cliff and in swamp it grows wild to this day. When they were on the march they would go in divisions. The work of the first division would be to clear the road of logs. The work of the second division would be to lower the hills. The work of the third division would be to sweep the path. Another division had to carry the sleds and the sleeping mats for the King. One division had charge of the food, and another division had charge of the planting of the crop. One division was composed of wizards and soothsayers and astrologers, and another division was made up of storytellers, fun makers, and musicians who made entertainment for the King. Some played on the nose flute, and others blew trumpets that were made by ripping a ti leaf away from the middle ridge and rolling over the torn piece. Through this they blew, varying the sound by fingering. They played stringed instruments that they held in their mouths, and they twanged the strings with their fingers. Others beat on drums that were hollow logs with shark skin drawn across them.

It would have been wonderful to look on the Me-ne-hu-ne when they were on the march. That would be on the nights of the full moon. Then they would all come together, and their King would speak to them.

And that reminds me of Ka-u-ki-u-ki, the Angry One. Perhaps he wanted to hold the legs of the Moon so that they might be able to listen a long time to their King, or march far in a night. I told you that he kept staring at the Owl of Ka-ne until the bird flew away in the night. But then it was too late to catch hold of the legs of the Moon. The next night he tried to do it. But although he stood on the top of the highest hill, and although he reached up to his fullest height, he could not lay hold on the legs of the Moon. And because he boasted of doing a thing that he could not do, the rest of the Me-ne-hu-ne punished him; they turned him into a stone. And a stone the Angry One is to this day—a stone on the top of the hill from which he tried to reach up and lay hold upon the legs of the Moon.

Perhaps it was on the very night which Ka-u-ki-u-ki tried to lengthen that their King told the Me-ne-hu-ne that they were to leave these islands. Some of the Me-ne-hu-ne had married Hawaiian women, and children that were half Me-ne-hu-ne and half Hawaiian were born. The King of the Me-ne-hu-ne folk did not like this: he wanted his people to remain pure Me-ne-hu-ne. So on a bright moonlit night he had them all come together, men, women, and children, and he spoke to them. "All of you," he said, "who have married wives from amongst the Hawaiian people must leave them, and all of the Me-ne-hu-ne race must go away from these Islands. The food that we planted in the valley is ripe; that food we will leave for the wives and children that we do not take with us—the Hawaiian women and the half-Hawaiian children."

When their King said this, no word was spoken for a long time from the ranks of the Me-ne-hu-ne. Then one whose name was Mo-hi-ki-a spoke up and said: "Must all of us go, O King, and may none of us stay with the Hawaiian wives that we have married? I have married an Hawaiian woman, and I have a son who is now grown to manhood. May he not go with you while I remain with my wife? He is stronger than I am. I have taught him all the skill that I possessed in the making of canoes. He can use the adz and make a canoe out of a tree trunk more quickly than any other of the Me-ne-hu-ne. And none of the Me-ne-hu-ne is so swift in the race as he is. Take my son in my place, and if it ever happens that the Me-ne-hu-ne need me, my son can run quickly for me and bring me back."

The King would not have Mo-hi-ki-a stay behind. "We start on our journey tomorrow night," he said. "All the Me-ne-hu-ne will leave the islands, and the crop that is now grown will be left for the women and children."

And so the Me-ne-hu-ne in their great force left our islands, and where they went there is none of us who know. Perhaps they went back to Kahiki-mo-e, for in Kahiki-mo-e they had been for a time before they came back to Hawaii. But not all of the Me-ne-hu-ne left the islands. Some stole away from their divisions and hid in hollow logs, and their descendants we have with us to this day. There are still many Me-ne-hu-ne away up in the mountains, living in caves and in hollow logs.

But the great force of them left the islands then. Before they went they made a monument. Upon the top of the highest hill they built it, carrying up the stones the night after the King had commanded them to leave. The monument was for the King and the Chiefs of the Me-ne-hu-ne—the monument of stones that we see. And for the Me-ne-hu-ne of common birth they made another monument. This they did by hollowing out a great cave in the mountain. The monument of stones on the top of the mountain and the cave in the side of the mountain you can see to this day.

On the next moonlit night the Me-ne-hu-ne in their thousands looked and saw the monuments they had raised. They were ready for the march as they looked, men and women, half-grown men and half-grown women, and little children. They looked and they saw the monument that they had raised on the mountain. Thereupon all the little men raised such a shout that the fish in the pond of No-mi-lu, at the other side of the island, jumped in fright, and the moi, the wary fish, left the beaches. And then, with trumpets sounding, flutes playing, and drums beating, the Me-ne-hu-ne started off.

O my younger brothers, I wish there were some amongst us, the Hawaiians of today, who knew the Me-ne-hu-ne of the mountains and who could go to them. All the work that it takes us so long to do, they could do in a night. Here we go every day to cut sandalwood for our King. We go away from our homes and our villages, leaving our crops unplanted and untended. We are up in the mountains by the first light of the morning, working, working with our axes to cut the sandalwood. And we go back at the fall of night carrying the loads of sandalwood upon our shoulders the whole way down the mountainside. Ah, if there were any amongst us who knew the Me-ne-hu-ne or who knew how to come to them! In one night the Me-ne-hu-ne would cut all the sandalwood for us! And the night after they would carry it down on their shoulders to the beach, where it would be put on the ships that would take it away to the land of the Pa-ke. But only those who are descendants of the Me-ne-hu-ne can come to them.

A long time ago a King ruled in Kau-ai whose name was Ola. His people were poor, for the river ran into the stony places and left their fields without water. "How can I bring water to my people?" said Ola the King to Pi, his wizard. "I will tell you how you can do it," Pi said. And then he told the King what to do so as to get the help of the Me-ne-hu-ne.

Pi, the wise man, went into the mountains. He was known to the Me-ne-hu-ne who had remained in the land, and he went before their Chief, and he asked him to have his people make a watercourse for Ola's people: they would have to dam the river with great stones and then make a trench that would carry the water down to the people's fields—a trench that would have stones fitted into its bed and fitted into its sides.

All the work that takes us days to do can be done by the Me-ne-hu-ne in the space of a night. And what they do not finish in a night is left unfinished. "*Ho po hookahi, a ao ua pau*," "In one night and it is finished," say the Me-ne-hu-ne.

Well, in one night all the stones for the dam and the water-course were made ready: one division went and gathered them, and another cut and shaped them. The stones were all left to-gether, and the Me-ne-hu-ne called them "the Pack of Pi."

Now King Ola had been told what he was to have done on the night that followed. There was to be no sound and there was to be no stir amongst his people. The dogs were to be muz-zled so that they could not bark, and the cocks and the hens were to be put into calabashes so that there should be no crowing from them. Also a feast was to be ready for the Me-ne-hu-ne.

Down from the mountain in the night came the troops of the Me-ne-hu-ne, each carrying a stone in his hand. Their trampling and the hum of their voices were heard by Pi as he stayed by the river; they were heard while they were still a long way off. They came down, and they made a trench with their digging tools of wood. Then they began to lay the stones at the bottom and along the sides of the trench; each stone fitted perfectly into its place. While one division was doing this the other division was building the dam across the river. The dam was built, the water was turned into the course, and Pi, standing there in the moonlight, saw the water come over the stones that the Me-ne-hu-ne had laid down.

Pi, and no one else, saw the Me-ne-hu-ne that night: half the size of our men they were, but broad across the chest and very strong. Pi admired the way they all worked together; they never got into each other's way, and they never waited for some one else to do something or to help them out. They finished their work just at daybreak; and then Pi gave them their feast. He gave a shrimp to each; they were well satisfied, and while it was still dark they departed. They crossed the watercourse that was now bringing water down to the people's taro patches.

And as they went the hum of their voices was so loud that it was heard in the distant island of Oahu. *"Wawa ka Menehune i Puukapele, ma Kauai, puoho ka manu o ka loko o Kawainui ma Koolaupoko, Oahu,"* our people said afterward. "The hum of the voices of the Me-ne-hu-ne at Pu-u-ka-pe-le, Kau-ai, startled the birds of the pond of Ka-wai-nui, at Ko'o-lau-po-ko, Oahu."

Look now! The others from our village are going down the mountainside, with the loads of sandalwood upon their backs. It is time we put our loads upon our shoulders and went likewise. As we go, I will tell you a story I know about the Me-ne-hu-ne.

There was once a boy of your age, O my younger brother, and his name was Laka. His father and mother went in the canoe across the Great Ocean and never afterward were they seen or heard of. The boy grew up in the house of his grandmother. He would often ask her about his father and mother, and the more he grew up the more often he asked about them. Then when he was as tall as you are he told his grandmother he would go across the sea in search of them. But he could not go until he had a canoe. "How am I to get a canoe?" he said to his grandmother one day.

"Go to the mountains and look for a tree that has leaves shaped like the new moon," said his grandmother. "Take your ax with you. When you find such a tree, cut it down, for it is the tree to make a canoe out of."

So Laka went to the mountains. He brought his ax with him. All day he searched in the woods, and at last he found a tree that had leaves shaped like the new moon. He commenced to cut through its trunk with his little ax of stone. At nightfall the trunk was cut through, and the tree fell down on the ground.

Then, well content with his day's work, Laka went back to his grandmother's. The next day he would cut off the branches and drag the trunk down to the beach and begin to make his canoe. He went back to the mountains. He searched and searched through all the woods, but he could find no trace of the tree that he had cut down with so much labor.

He went to the mountains again the day after. He found another tree growing with leaves shaped like the new moon. With his little stone ax he cut through the trunk, and the tree fell down. Then he went back to his grandmother's, thinking that he would go the next day and cut off the branches and bring the trunk down to the beach.

But the next day when he went to the mountains there was no trace of the tree that he had cut down with so much labor. He searched for it all day, but could not find it. The next day he had to begin his labor all over again: he had to search for a tree that had leaves like the new moon, he had to cut through the trunk and let it lie on the ground. After he had cut down the third tree he spoke to his grandmother about the trees that he had cut and had lost sight of. His wise grandmother told him that if the third tree disappeared, he was to dig a trench beside where the next tree would fall. And when that tree came down he was to hide in the trench beside it and watch what would happen.

When Laka went up to the mountain the next day he found that the tree he had cut was lost to his sight like the others. He found another tree with leaves shaped like the new moon. He began to cut this one down. Near where it would fall he dug a trench.

It was very late in the evening when he cut through this tree. The trunk fell, and it covered the trench he had made. Then Laka went under and hid himself. He waited while the night came on.

Then, while he was waiting, he heard the hum of voices, and he knew that a band of people were drawing near. They were singing as they came on. Laka heard what they sang.

> "O the four thousand gods,
> O the forty thousand gods,
> O the four hundred thousand gods,
> O the file of gods,
> O the assembly of gods!
> O gods of these woods,
> Of the mountain, the knoll,
> Of the dam of the watercourse, O descend!"

Then there was more noise, and Laka, looking up from the trench, saw that the clearing around him was all filled with a crowd of little men. They came where the tree lay, and they tried to move it. Then Laka jumped out of the trench, and he laid hands upon one of the little people. He threatened to kill him for having moved away the trees he had cut.

As he jumped up all the little people disappeared. Laka was left with the one he held.

"Do not kill me," said the little man. "I am of the Me-ne-hu-ne, and we intend no harm to you. I will say this to you: if you kill me, there will be no one to make the canoe for you, no one to drag it down to the beach, making it ready for you to sail in. If you do not kill me, my friends will make the canoe for you. And if you build a shed for it, we will bring the canoe finished to you and place it in the shed."

Then Laka said he would gladly spare the little man if he and his friends would make the canoe for him and bring it down to the shed that he would make. He let the little man go then. The next day he built a shed for the canoe.

When he told his grandmother about the crowd of little men he had seen and about the little man he had caught, she told him that they were the Me-ne-hu-ne, who lived in hollow logs and in caves in the mountains. No one knew how many of them there were.

He went back, and he found that where the trunk of the tree had lain there was now a canoe perfectly finished; all was there that should be there, even to the light, well-shaped paddle, and all had been finished in the night. He went back, and that night he waited beside the shed which he had built out on the beach. At the dead of the night he heard the hum of voices. That was when the canoe was being lifted up. Then he heard a second hum of voices. That was when the canoe was being carried on the hands of the Me-ne-hu-ne—for they did not drag the canoe, they carried it. He heard a trampling of feet. Then he heard a third hum of voices; that was when the canoe was being let down in the shed he had built.

Laka's grandmother, knowing who they were, had left a feast for the Me-ne-hu-ne—a shrimp for each, and some cooked taro leaves. They ate, and before it was daylight they returned to the mountain where their caves were. The boy Laka saw the Me-ne-hu-ne as they went up the side of the mountain—hundreds of little men tramping away in the waning darkness.

His canoe was ready, paddle and all. He took it down to the sea, and he went across in search of his father. When he landed on the other side he found a wise man who was able to tell him about his father, and that he was dead indeed, having been killed by a very wicked man on his landing. The boy never went back to his grandmother's. He stayed, and with the canoe that the Me-ne-hu-ne had made for him he became a famous fisherman. From him have come my fathers and your fathers, too, O my younger brothers.

And you who are the youngest and littlest of all—gather you the ku-kui nuts as we go down; tonight we will make strings of them and burn them, lighting the house. And if we have many ku-kui nuts and a light that is long-lasting, it may be that you will hear more stories.

THE CANOE OF
LAKA OR RATA

AND THOSE WHO SAILED IN IT

A pathway for the canoe! A pathway for the canoe!
A pathway of sweet-scented flowers for the canoe!
A pathway to the sea!

SUCH was the chant that Laka whom we in the Southern
Seas name Rata, heard from those who were bringing
him the canoe.

He had got his tools together and was prepared to go into the
forest to hollow out the tree he had cut down when he heard the
chant. He saw the canoe outside; it was beautifully finished and
he knew that gods or godlings had finished it for him and had
sent it to him there. He named the canoe Tarai-po, "Built-in-a-
Night." It was in this canoe that Rata sailed across the ocean to
take vengeance on the Children of Puna who had devoured his
father and his mother.

How Rata Sailed Across the Sea in His Canoe and How Vengeance Was Taken upon the Children of Puna and upon Puna Himself.

WHEN she saw the canoe that was so beautifully shaped, Kui,
his grandmother, said to him: "It is well for you, my grandson;
the gods have made your canoe for you, and you will become a
famous man, and your descendants will be many. But your first
deeds must be the deeds of vengeance you wreak on the Children
of Puna; do not spare them."

He tried his canoe upon the lagoon to see if it sailed well. It
sailed better than any canoe that had ever before been seen

there. But Rata had at this time no men to sail with him in the canoe.

Then a man came to him and called out, "O Rata, where are you going?" "I am going to sail over the ocean and avenge the deaths of my father and my mother." The man said, "I will go with you." "Who are you?" "I am Canoe-Paddler." "Come on board, Canoe-Paddler," said Rata.

Another man came, and he said, "O Rata, where are you going?" "I am going to sail over the ocean to avenge the deaths of my mother and my father." "I will go with you." "Who are you?" "I am Rope-Worker." "Come on board, Rope-Worker," said Rata.

And then another man came, and another. "Who are you?" "I am Sail-Maker." "Come on board, Sail-Maker." "I am Canoe-Bailer." "Come on board, Canoe-Bailer."

Another came, and another, and another. "Who are you?" "I am Sailing-Master." "I am Paddle-Maker." "I am Canoe-Steerer." When they were all on board Rata had his crew of seven men. They set up the sail, they took up the paddles, and they were ready to sail across the ocean to take vengeance on the Children of Puna.

Just as they were ready to start off another man came, and asked to be taken aboard the canoe. "Who are you?" said Rata. "I am Nanoa." "What do you do, Nanoa?" "I fly kites." "You fly kites, and what then?" "I fly kites and I exalt the heavens in my song." "I will not take you on board."

The canoe started off. Then out in the middle of the sea the people of the canoe came upon a great calabash floating. "Our calabash of good luck," said the men, "we will take it into the canoe." They took it into the canoe and a voice spoke out of it, "O Rata." "This is Nanoa, the flyer of kites," said Rata, "into the sea with him." So they threw the calabash into the sea again.

They sailed on. Out in the middle of the ocean they saw a great calabash floating. "Our calabash of good luck," said the men. They took it into the canoe. They opened it, and there was Nanoa. This time Rata let Nanoa stay in the canoe.

As they went over the boundless ocean, Nanoa cried out, "There is death before us!" They looked and they saw a monster before them on the sea. "Declare now who is your wizard," Nanoa said. "We have no wizard; you, Nanoa, are our wizard," Rata said. "You have made me your wizard; now I will strive for you against the terrible Children of Puna and against Puna himself," said Nanoa.

Before them was the first of the Children of Puna—Eke, the Octopus. Its eyes were on a level with the surface of the sea; one of its tentacles gripped the bed of the ocean; another of its tentacles was raised up to the sky; when it descended it would break the canoe and crush all the men in it.

Nanoa went into his calabash, and he made it float over to where the Octopus was. It put its tentacles around the calabash; it took the calabash into its mouth. But Nanoa had his knife in his hand; he attacked its heart. Eke the Octopus thrashed the sea with its tentacles, and it poured out its blackness upon the waters. But in a while it sank down from the surface of the sea. The people in the canoe thought Nanoa was lost to them, but then they saw the calabash floating on the water. They took it into the canoe, and Nanoa came out of it uninjured. "But for you, O Nanoa, we should all have been destroyed," Rata said to him.

They went on in the boundless ocean, and then Nanoa cried out again, "There is death before us!" They looked, and they saw a great clam, with its shell open ready to draw them in. This was Pa-ua the Clam, the second of the Children of Puna. Nanoa went into his calabash again; he made it float over to where the Clam was. The Clam took the calabash into its shell, and sank with it down to the bottom of the ocean. Rata thought their helper was lost to them. But in a while the calabash came to the surface of the sea again; they took it into the canoe, and when they opened it, Nanoa was there uninjured; he had killed the Clam at the bottom of the ocean, and had forced his way out of its shell.

Again they went on through the boundless ocean. "There is death before us!" Nanoa cried out. And now they saw Mano-a the Great Shark bearing down upon them. Nanoa got into his calabash; it floated and the Shark came to it. Mano-a tried to take the calabash between its double row of teeth, but the calabash spun round and round and he could not bite at it.

Nanoa slipped out of his calabash. He plunged into the shark's mouth, past the double rows of teeth. He had his knife in his hands, and he struck at the Shark's heart with it. He came out of the Shark's mouth again, and Mano-a, the third of the Children of Puna, floated upon the water, dead.

Nanoa came into the canoe. "But for you, O Nanoa, we should all have been destroyed," Rata said to him. The canoe went on over the boundless ocean, toward the Island where Puna lived.

Again Nanoa cried out, "There is death ahead of us!" They saw, bearing down upon them, the last of the Children of Puna, Aku the Swordfish. He came charging at them. Nanoa turned the canoe until it lay with its side before Aku. He charged it, and the sword which was the whole length of Aku's lower jaw was embedded in the canoe. His mouth was left open. He lifted the canoe up with his lower jaw and tried to shake it off. But now Nanoa dived under the water and stabbed up at Aku with his knife. The monster shook the canoe this way and that way, sweeping it through the sea and lifting it up in the air. The men cut through the lower jaw with their axes, and Aku was left floating on the sea. Thus the last of the Children of Puna was destroyed. "But for you, O Nanoa, we should have been destroyed," said Rata to his wizard.

They sailed for the island where Puna lived. "Do not go upon the island until the cold south wind blows," Nanoa told

Rata. "Puna is weak when the cold comes." So they did not go upon the island until they felt the cold of the south wind.

And when they went on the island Nanoa went before them to the place where Puna was. He was weak at the time, and Nanoa was able to bind his hands to the trees and his feet to the rocks. So Puna was bound when Rata came to him.

And when he saw the youth, Puna said: "Begone! I am old, but tomorrow I will show you that I am able to overcome you." "I am Rata," said the youth, "and I have come to take vengeance on you for the deaths of my father and my mother." Then Puna started up; he broke the trees that held his hands; he split the rocks that held his feet. The sun rose, and Puna was overthrown; Rata left him there dead.

And having avenged on the Children of Puna and on Puna himself the deaths of his father and mother, Rata, after visiting many islands, sailed back to his home. "Here am I," he cried, "the warrior who went into the deep sea, the splashing sea, and who returned safely after having taken vengeance on those who killed my mother and my father." And Kui, his grandmother, said to him, "O thrice powerful thou art; great is thy strength and great are thy deeds; I behold thee now, not as a man, but as an immortal."

How Rata Came to His Death.

WOULD you hear how Rata, our great ancestor, came to his death—Rata who made so many voyages and planted his people upon so many islands that people had not gone on before— Rata who traveled throughout all the Great Engulfing Ocean in the canoe that the gods had given him—would you hear how Rata came to his death at last?

In the Island of Manuka there lived a giant chief whose name was Vaea. Vaea heard that Rata was coming to his island. He went down to the beach to watch for the strange canoe.

It came in. Night fell and the men drew the canoe up on the

beach and went to sleep in it—Rata and all his men. Then Vaea, that giant chief, went down to where the canoe was drawn up. He lifted it; he carried it over the mountains in the dark night, the canoe with the sleeping men in it, and he left it in the tops of the trees.

Before the dawn came the Canoe-Bailer awakened. He took up his bailing vessel and began to empty out the water that was in the canoe. He heard the water fall. But it did not splash as if it fell upon water; as he flung the water out of the canoe it sounded like rain.

Then the Bailer looked over the edge of the canoe. He saw the tree tops. He saw that the canoe was in the tops of trees. He called out and he awakened Rata and the men.

All around them was the forest, and they, in their canoe, were on the tops of the forest trees. Into what strange land had they come? The sun mounted in the sky, and the men who had crossed the boundless ocean looked all around them, and they saw nothing but the forests of a strange country. One by one they began to climb down the trees.

And as they came down, Vaea the chief of the Island, killed them one by one. Last of all Rata came down. He had the ropes of the canoe; he pulled them, and he made the canoe fall through the branches and come down upon the ground.

Then Rata and Vaea strove together, and Rata was the one who was slain. Later Apa-kura, the wife of Vaea, came searching in the forest for her husband. She found him beside Rata's canoe that was now turned into stone. And Vaea was half turned to stone. As she came to him he said, "Come, my companion. I, Vaea, the slayer of Rata, go down into the shades." He fell down, a stony man beside the stone canoe. The place where all this happened is called to this day "Te Vao rakau o Rata," "The Forest of Rata's Canoe."

And there are stories that tell more about Apa-kura; in these stories she did not go down to the shades with Vaea, her husband. A youth came in from the sea who was Tu-whaka-raro, the son of Rata. He took Apa-kura for his wife, and their son was Whaka-tau, who for a long time lived under the sea, and flew kites, and knew magic.

WHEN THE
LITTLE BLOND
SHARK WENT
VISITING

KAPU-KAPU was the father and Ho-lei was the mother
of the Little Blond Shark—Ka-ehu-iki, he was called.
He asked his parents' permission to go visiting; his
mother was fearful on account of the dangers he might en-
counter, but his father reassured her, saying that no dangers
would befall their child while he went visiting his relatives and
making a tour through the wide ocean.

Kapu-kapu gave him permission to go, and he gave his child,
too, advice that would last him until he came to where Ka-
moho-ali'i was—Ka-moho-ali'i, the King of All the Sharks.
And the Little Blond Shark asked his father to tell him the
names of the king-sharks in the waters around, so that he might

call on them and pay his respects to them. Kapu-kapu then chanted their names:

"Ka-panila, the King-Shark of Hilo,
And Kaneilehia, the King-Shark of Kau;
Mano-kini, the King-Shark of Kohala,
Ka-pu-lena, the King-Shark of Hamakua,
And Kua, the King-Shark of Kona."

And when he had heard these names Ka-ehu-iki, the Little Blond Shark, started off.

The first one he called on was the King-Shark of Hilo. "Is the stranger on a journey for pleasure?" said Ka-panila to him when he appeared at his cave at Hilo. "For pleasure, and to obtain instruction and some knowledge of the world," said the Little Blond Shark.

This reply pleased Ka-panila, and he bade the youthful stranger enter his cave. Ka-ehu-iki came within, and the two talked and ate together. "I am now setting forth," said the Little Blond Shark; "but would you, my lord and my chief, consent to add dignity to my tour by being my companion on the way?"

The King-Shark of Hilo consented, and in the morning the two started off together. They came to Kau. At first the King-Shark of Kau treated them distantly, but in a while he was made friendly by the manners and the address of the Little Blond Shark. And when they started off in the morning Kaneile-hia of Kau had consented to accompany them.

They went on to Kona, to Kohala, and to Hamakua. The Little Blond Shark introduced the Kings to each other, and he prevailed upon each of them to join in the tour he was making.

And so they went on, a friendly and a fine-looking company of sharks, full of good will for everyone and everything and admired by all who saw them. Mano-kini of Kohala was the one who had been hardest to win over. But he agreed to go with them when he heard that it was their youthful leader's intention to proceed to Tahiti. "Muli-wai-lena, the Yellow River of Tahiti!" he said; "I will go until I bathe in it." But he warned the rest that they would have to be careful in going through the channel near Hana, for the rough King Kau-huhu's general kept guard there.

"Perhaps he is warlike only when one approaches him in a warlike way," said the Little Blond Shark.

"Whether we approach him in a warlike or in a peaceable way he will try to bar our passage," said Mano-kini.

"Very well," said the Little Blond Shark; "but I on my part will not forget that I am the offspring of Kapu-kapu, the guard of Panau, who never turned his back on a battle offered him. I will not forget that," said the Little Blond Shark.

At these words the Kings who were with him looked at each other and nudged each other. "The high blood will show, the high blood will show," they said.

When they entered the channel at Hana they were met by a line of ocean battlers, the rough guards of the rough King Kau-huhu. The guards challenged Ka-ehu-iki and his party. The Little Blond Shark told them that they were on a journey of pleasure, and that they were going to no nearer place than Tahiti.

"You're not going through King Kau-huhu's channel, anyway," said one of these rough ones.

"Why should we not?" asked the Little Blond Shark with dignity.

"If you attempt to cross this way, it will be war—do you hear that?" said the head guardsman.

"It is singular to hear you speak in such a way," said the Little Blond Shark. "You could not be more truculent if we had come here to make war."

"War it will be," said King Kau-huhu's head guardsman, "if any of you attempt to come in on these borders."

Then the Little Blond Shark called his companions, each by his name, his title, and his kingship, and spoke to them. "There is but one way," he said, "and that is the way that is marked out by our own strength and bravery. You remain outside the channel," he said to his friends, "and if I should fail in this, the way is open for your return to your native waters."

Having said this, the Little Blond Shark went forward and challenged King Kau-huhu's head guardsman. The great shark mocked at him, saying that a battle with such an undersized crab would only be a pastime for him. The Little Blond Shark went toward him. The guardsman made ready. As he did so Ka-ehu-iki shot forward and seized him by the fins; he held the fins fast. The great shark went this way and that way, and up and down, but Ka-ehu-iki went this way and that way with him, and up and down, without ever letting go his hold. He bit and bit at the great shark, and at last he bit through him. Then all the watching sharks saw the channel's great guardsman float away dead.

They were all amazed at the strength and bravery shown by the Little Blond Shark. They went to him and praised him and told him they would have him for their leader. Then they went to the cave where that rough shark, King Kau-huhu, lived.

Instead of welcoming his visitors King Kau-huhu looked at them angrily. And the words he said were so cold and distant that Ka-ehu-iki was moved to say to him:

"Well indeed does your angry name befit you, King Kau-huhu; in no other royal cave that we have come to have we had such an unfriendly reception."

Kau-huhu was made more and more angry by the address of the Little Blond Shark, and he immediately challenged the youngster to battle. Ka-ehu-iki called his companions, each by his name, his title, and his kingship, and he said to them: "Stay near and watch the battle. If I am overcome the way is open for your return to your native waters, and if I am victor we will celebrate my day together."

Kau-huhu was impatient for the battle; without waiting for the Little Blond Shark to take up a position, he rushed out at him, coming into the open with his jaws extended as if to take in everything in the ocean. Ka-ehu-iki slipped out of his way; then he caught at his fins and held them until Kau-huhu was wearied out. And then the Little Blond Shark bit through the surly King and left him to float off dead.

He called to his companions; they came forward and congratulated him on his victory; then they went through the channel, making their way to the cave of Ka-moho-ali'i, the King of All the Sharks.

When they came before his cave they sent a respectful message to him within, informing the King of All the Sharks that they were on a peaceful tour of sight-seeing, and begging permission to wait upon him.

The guard came back, and Ka-ehu-iki and his friends were brought within a splendid cave where they were entertained and given a magnificent banquet. Then they were taken before the King of All the Sharks.

Ka-moho-ali'i appeared before them, a most impressive figure; he was all overgrown with barnacles, and sea mosses were streaming down from him. All the visiting sharks admired their great and venerable King.

Ka-ehu-iki addressed him, introducing each of his companions by his name, his title, and his kingship. He explained the object of his journey. And then he prayed that Ka-moho-ali'i might adopt him as his grandchild. The King of All the Sharks was pleased with the appearance of the Little Blond Shark and with all he said, and he freely agreed to adopt him as his grandchild. He had Ka-ehu-iki anointed as a king is anointed.

"Ka-moho-ali'i sets the seal of his approval on you with this anointing," said the attendant, "and he grants you power second to none in all this broad ocean, from north to south, from east to west, and wherever your travels may take you, and none may triumph over you from one horizon to the other, even to the borders of Tahiti. And those who might challenge you will know by these presents that quietness will be their safety and contentions will be their death."

They rested until next day in Ka-moho-ali'i's cave; at parting the King of All the Sharks gave the youthful leader his blessing. Ka-ehu-iki replied, "O King of the Sharks of this wide Ocean, we leave our humble and hearty thanks with you for the good will you have shown us, and we shall carry as far as the sacred crossroad of Nu'u-mea-lani and back the memory of your royal kindness to us."

Then they went to call upon Ka-ahu-pahau, the Queen-Shark of the waters. By a circuitous route they were taken to her cave and they were presented to the Queen and all her court. Almost immediately they were asked to join a bathing party that the Queen was taking to Wai-mano; they went, and they greatly enjoyed the waters there.

Afterward they went back to the royal cave, where they were entertained by various games—*kilu* and *puili*. And there Ka-panila, the King-Shark of Hilo, for the Queen's entertainment, chanted the legends of Hawaii that were known from the most ancient times.

At the end of ten days, when they were making ready to start on their journey, the Queen presented the youthful leader with her own ivory wreath; with this in his possession he would be recognized and accepted by the guardian sharks of all the royal domains. She begged him to take a competent pilot with their party, one who knew the way to Tahiti and the way back. Ka-ehu-iki agreed to do this; Kua of Kona, who was originally from Tahiti, who knew its waters, and who had relatives still there, was the one chosen for pilot.

Under the guidance of Kua they came into the waters of Tahiti. They bathed in Muli-wai-lena, the Yellow River of Tahiti; they met and they conversed with their giant relatives. And, everywhere they went, the ivory wreath presented to Ka-ehu-iki by the Queen-Shark won friendship for them.

They bathed in Muli-wai-lena, the Yellow River of Tahiti, for the last time, and then they started for their home waters. When they were near the islands they were met by a very degraded shark who thought the Ka-ehu-iki and all his company were of the same kind as himself. He proposed to the Little Blond Shark that they should go and attack human beings when they were surf riding.

"Indeed," said Ka-ehu-iki, "and may we know who it is who makes this fine proposal?"

"I am Pehu," said this offensive shark.

"From where do you come, Pehu?" asked Ka-ehu-iki.

"From Hono-ko-hau," the fellow said. "Let us go and catch crabs," said he then, meaning by that that he would have them go and catch human beings.

The Little Blond Shark pretended to fall in with the fellow's proposals. He said to him: "We know how to come on these human beings. Follow us to the place where they are surf riding." Pehu then followed them, and they all went on.

But Ka-ehu-iki said to Ka-panila, the King-Shark of Hilo, who was beside him: "This degraded fellow would bring trouble upon Ka-ahu-pahau, the Queen-Shark of these waters who was so hospitable to us, for if any man-eating took place here she would be blamed for it. We will have to do something to bring his career to an end." He went back to Pehu and said to him: "Follow us to the place that the surf riders start from. You go shoreward while we remain seaward. We will watch for you, and when we give you the signal you can seize on one of the human beings." Pehu agreed to this, and then Ka-ehu-iki said to Ka-panila: "Let us lead this Pehu to his death. Let us crowd in on him when he comes near the shallow place and force him in on it." All Ka-ehu-iki's companions agreed to do it.

That day the surf was breaking strong, and there were many human beings at the outer surf line. The sharks all went in a quiet manner until they were close to where the human beings took the bursting wave. Pehu said, "Let us make a seizure now." "No," said Ka-ehu-iki, "wait until they take the surf. Then let us all rush in together. We will be in the swell of the surf, and when I cry out to you, that will be the time to make the seizure." Pehu went on then, but he waited for the signal from Ka-ehu-iki.

Presently the surf rose, and two human beings rode on it shoreward. The sharks swam with them. And when they were near the shallows the Little Blond Shark gave the word to his companions. They crowded in on Pehu. He heard the signal that he waited for. He leaped forward and sunk his head in a coral crevice, and his tail stood up in the air. Then Ka-ehu-iki and his companions went back into the deep water.

When the human beings who were surf riding caught a glimpse of the sharks they were greatly terrified, and they fled ashore. Later on they came back; they took the carcass of Pehu and they burned the degraded shark to ashes.

The Little Blond Shark and his companions went then to their home waters. Ka-panila of Hilo went with Ka-ehu-iki to Panau, where his parents were. You may be sure that Kapu-kapu was delighted to see his son so well-grown, so polished, too, by his travels, and so well commended by the Kings who had consented to join in his tour. He made a feast to welcome him home. For his mother and father it was a proud occasion when Ka-ehu-iki conveyed to them the royal greetings that had been given him for them, and the kind remembrances of so many distinguished sharks. Ka-panila told Kapu-kapu and Ho-lei of the great receptions that had been given them, and of Ka-ehu-iki's victories in battle. It was a tale that went on for many days.

THE BOY PU-NIA

AND THE KING OF THE SHARKS

O N one side of the island there lived a great shark: Kai-ale-ale he was named; he was the King of the Sharks of that place, and he had ten sharks under him. He lived near a cave that was filled with lobsters. But no one dared to dive down, and go into that cave, and take lobsters out of it, on account of Kai-ale-ale and the ten sharks he had under him; they stayed around the cave night and day, and if a diver ventured near they would bite him and devour him.

There was a boy named Pu-nia, whose father had been killed by the sharks. Now after his father had been killed, there was no one to catch fish for Pu-nia and his mother; they had sweet potatoes to eat, but they never had any fish to eat with them. Often Pu-nia heard his mother say that she wished she had a fish or lobster to eat with the sweet potatoes. He made up his mind that they should have lobsters.

He came above the cave where the lobsters were. Looking down he saw the sharks—Kai-ale-ale and his ten sharks; they were all asleep. While he was watching them, they wakened up. Pu-nia pretended that he did not know that the sharks had wakened. He spoke loudly so that they would hear him, and he said: "Here am I, Pu-nia, and I am going into the cave to get lobsters for myself and my mother. That great shark, Kai-ale-ale, is asleep now, and I can dive to the point over there, and then go into the cave; I will take two lobsters in my hands, and my mother and I will have something to eat with our sweet potatoes." So Pu-nia said, speaking loudly and pretending that he thought the sharks were still asleep.

Said Kai-ale-ale, speaking softly to the other sharks: "Let us rush to the place where Pu-nia dives, and let us devour him as we devoured his father." But Pu-nia was a very cunning boy and not at all the sort that could be caught by the stupid sharks.

He had a stone upon his hand while he was speaking, and he flung it toward the point that he said he was going to dive to. Just as soon as the stone struck the water the sharks made a rush to the place, leaving the cave of the lobsters unguarded. Then Pu-nia dived. He went into the cave, took two lobsters in his hands, and came up on the place that he had spoken from before.

He shouted down to the sharks: "Here is Pu-nia, and he has come back safely. He has two lobsters, and he and his mother have something to live on. It was the first shark, the second shark, the third shark, the fourth shark, the fifth shark, the sixth shark, the seventh shark, the eighth shark, the ninth shark, the tenth shark—it was the tenth shark, the one with the thin tail, that showed Pu-nia what to do."

When the King of the Sharks, Kai-ale-ale, heard this from Pu-nia, he ordered all the sharks to come together and stay in a row. He counted them, and there were ten of them, and the tenth one had a thin tail. "So it was you, Thin Tail," he said, "that told the boy Pu-nia what to do. You shall die." Then, according to the orders of Kai-ale-ale, the thin-tailed shark was killed. Pu-nia called out to them, "You have killed one of your own kind." With the two lobsters in his hands, he went back to his mother's.

Pu-nia and his mother now had something to eat with their sweet potatoes. And when the lobsters were all eaten, Pu-nia went back to the place above the cave. He called out, as he had done the first time: "I can dive to the place over there and then slip into the cave, for the sharks are all asleep; I can get two lobsters for myself and my mother, so that we'll have something to eat with our sweet potatoes." Then he threw down a stone and made ready to dive to another point.

When the stone struck the water the sharks rushed over, leaving the cave unguarded. Then Pu-nia dived down and went into the cave. He took two lobsters in his hands and swam back to the top of the water, and when he got to the place that he had spoken from before, he shouted down to the sharks: "It was the first shark, the second shark, the third shark, the fourth shark, the fifth shark, the sixth shark, the seventh shark, the eighth shark, the ninth shark—it was the ninth shark, the one with the big stomach, that told Pu-nia what to do."

Then the King of the Sharks, Kai-ale-ale, ordered the sharks to get into a line. He counted them, and he found that the ninth shark had a big stomach. "So it was you that told Pu-nia what to do," he said; and he ordered the big-stomached shark to be killed. After that Pu-nia went home with his two lobsters, and he and his mother had something to eat with their sweet potatoes.

Pu-nia continued to do this. He would deceive the sharks by throwing a stone to the place that he said he was going to dive to; when he got the sharks away from the cave, he would dive down, slip in, and take two lobsters in his hands. And always, when he got to the top of the water, he would name a shark. "The first shark, the second shark, the third shark—the shark with the little eye, the shark with the grey spot on him—told Pu-nia what to do," he would say; and each time he would get one of the sharks killed. He kept on doing this until only one of the sharks was left; this one was Kai-ale-ale, the King of the Sharks.

After that, Pu-nia went into the forest; he hewed out two hard pieces of wood, each about a yard long; then he took sticks for lighting a fire—the au-li-ma to rub with, and the au-na-ki to rub on; he got charcoal to burn as a fire, and he got food. He put all into a bag, and he carried the bag down to the beach. He came above the cave that Kai-ale-ale was watching, and he said, speaking in a loud voice: "If I dive now, and if Kai-ale-ale bites me, my blood will come to the top of the water, and my mother will see the blood and will bring me back to life again. But if I dive down and Kai-ale-ale takes me into his mouth whole, I shall die and never come back to life again." Kai-ale-ale was listening, of course. He said to himself: "No, I will not bite you, you cunning boy; I will take you into my mouth and swallow you whole, and then you will never come back to life again. I shall open my mouth wide enough to take you in. Yes, indeed, this time I will get you."

Pu-nia dived holding his bag. Kai-ale-ale opened his mouth wide and got Pu-nia into it. But as soon as the boy got within, he opened his bag and took out the two pieces of wood which he had hewn out in the forest. He put them between the jaws of the shark so that Kai-ale-ale was not able to close his jaws. With his mouth held open, Kai-ale-ale went dashing through the water.

Pu-nia was now inside the big shark; he took the fire sticks out of his bag and rubbed them together, making a fire. He kindled the charcoal that he had brought, and he cooked his food at the fire that he had made. With the fire in his insides, the shark could not keep still; he went dashing here and there through the ocean.

At last the shark came near the Island of Hawaii again. "If he brings me near the breakers, I am saved," said Pu-nia, speaking aloud; "but if he takes me to the sand near where the grass grows, I shall die; I cannot be saved." Kai-ale-ale, when he heard Pu-nia say this, said to himself: "I will not take him near the breakers; I will take him where the dry sand is, near the grass." Saying this, he dashed in from the ocean and up to where the shrubs grew on the shore. No shark had ever gone there before; and when Kai-ale-ale got there, he could not get back again.

Then Pu-nia came out of the shark. He shouted out, "Kai-ale-ale, Kai-ale-ale, the King of the Sharks, has come to visit us." And the people, hearing about their enemy Kai-ale-ale, came down to the shore with their spears and their knives and killed him. And that was the end of the ugly and wicked King of the Sharks.

Every day after that, Pu-nia was able to go down into the cave and get lobsters for himself and his mother. And all the people rejoiced when they knew that the eleven sharks that guarded the cave had been got rid of by the boy Pu-nia.

OWL AND RAT

AND THE BOY WHO WAS GOOD AT SHOOTING ARROWS

OWL was a farmer and Rat was a thief. They lived for a while as friends, but Owl got to know about Rat's ways and gave up keeping company with him. Owl was very upright: he worked every night on his farm in Ko-ha-la, and when the sun rose he rested, for his eyes became tired then. Rat had no scruples about going on Owl's potato patch and stealing what Owl had cultivated. He did this so bare-facedly that Owl caught him at his thieveries more than eight times. After that Rat went to the potato patch only in the day-time; Owl had to keep his eyes open so that he could follow him and pounce upon him in the potato patch or when he was going to it or coming from it. Once he nearly got his claws into him. And after that Owl no longer saw Rat going to or coming from his potato patch.

That was because Rat didn't go openly there any more. He dug a passage underground. It went from his own house to

Owl's potato patch. No one would see him go there, and I-o-le the Rat would stay all day eating Pu-e-o the Owl's potatoes. Then, one night Owl went to get some potatoes for himself. Instead of the good crop that he expected to find, there were no potatoes at all on one side of the patch, and on the other side there were only stalks with bits of potatoes at the ends of them.

Then Owl knew that Rat had tricked him and had thieved from him again. His eyes blazed more than an owl's ever blazed before, so angry he was. And he got more red-eyed than an owl was ever before, because he wept all day to think that that low fellow Rat was going up and down and taking his ease as though he wasn't to be blamed for anything, while he, Pu-e-o, was hungry and disappointed. He went to I-o the Hawk about it. But Hawk, though he was the strongest of all the animals, would do nothing against one who was so cunning as Rat. However, he told him about a boy who was good at shooting arrows, Pi-ko-i, the Son of Crow. Owl went to him and made friends with him, and told Crow's son where there was a good mark for his arrow. And now Owl has his patch of potatoes all to himself. For as Rat was placidly dreaming in the long grass, Pi-ko-i, the Son of Crow, shot an arrow that went all the way from his forehead to his tail.

At that time Pi-ko-i had a sharp face, his bones were little, and he had hair that was like a rat's. "Where were you born and who are your parents?" two women asked him when he went into a house that Owl had told him about. "I am from Wai-lua on the Island of Kau-ai; Ala-la the Crow is my father and Kou-kou is my mother."

When he told them this, the women knew who he was, and they cried over their brother. Then their husbands came home, and a great feast was prepared for Pi-ko-i. A pig was killed, yams were made ready, and pig and yams were put into the underground oven to cook. But while the cooking was being done, Pi-ko-i left the house and wandered off to where there was a crowd, and where games were being played.

The Chief and Chieftainess were at these games. A game of shooting was on; a man was shooting arrows at rats, and the Chief and Chieftainess were laying wagers on his shooting.

It was a Prince who was shooting arrows at the rats—Mai-ne-le was his name—and all thought that his aim was most wonderful. The Chief was winning all her property from the Chieftainess, for he was laying wagers all the time on Mai-ne-le's shooting.

Pi-ko-i stood and watched the game for a while. After the Prince had shot several arrows he said: "How simple all this is! Why, anyone could shoot as this man shoots." When the Chieftainess heard the stranger boy say this, she said, "Could you shoot as well as the Prince?" "Yes, ma'am," said Pi-ko-i. "Then I will wager my property on your shooting," said the Chieftainess.

The Chief kept on staking his property on the Prince's shooting, while the Chieftainess now staked hers on Pi-ko-i's. Whoever should strike ten rats with one arrow would win, and whoever should strike less than ten would lose the match. Prince Mai-ne-le shot first. His arrow went through ten rats, and all the people shouted, "Mai-ne-le has won, Mai-ne-le has won! The stranger boy cannot do better than that!" But Pi-ko-i only said, "How left-handed that man must be! I thought that he was going to shoot the rats through their whiskers!"

Prince Mai-ne-le heard what Pi-ko-i said, and he answered angrily: "You are a deceiving boy. From the first day I began shooting rats until this day, I have never seen a man who could shoot rats through their whiskers." "You will see one now," said Pi-ko-i.

Then bets were made as to whether one could shoot through rats' whiskers. These were new bets, and when they were all made, Pi-ko-i made ready to shoot. But now the rats were all gone; not one was in sight. Thereupon Pi-ko-i said a charm to bring the rats near:

> "I, Pi-ko-i,
> The offspring of Ala-la the Crow
> The offspring of Kou-kou:
> Where are you, my brothers?
> Where are you, O Rats?
> There they are,
> There they are!
> The rats are in the pili grass:
> They sleep, the rats are asleep:
> Let them awaken;
> Let them return!"

And when he said this charm the rats all came back. Pi-ko-i then let his arrow fly. It struck ten rats, and the point of it held a bat. The rats were all made fast by their whiskers.

When Mai-ne-le saw this he said: "It is a draw. The boy shot ten rats, and I shot ten rats." The people all agreed with Mai-ne-le—it was a draw, they said. But Pi-ko-i would not have it so. "The bat must count as a rat," he said. "I have killed, not ten, but eleven rats." The crowd would not agree. Pi-ko-i kept saying, "It counts as a rat according to the old words:

> " 'The bat is in the stormless season—
> He is your younger brother, O Rat:
> Squeak to him.' "

And when he said that, everyone had to agree that the bat counted as a rat and that Pi-ko-i had killed eleven rats with his single arrow. And so he won the match against Prince Mai-ne-le.

While the wagers were being handed over, Pi-ko-i slipped away. He went back to his sisters' house; he was there as the food was being taken out of the oven. He sat down to the food; he would not let anyone speak to him while he ate. He ate nearly the whole ovenful. And when he had finished that meal he was a changed boy: he was no longer sharp faced and small boned; he still had hair like rat's hair, but for all that he was now a fine-looking youth.

Shortly after this the Chief and Chieftainess wanted to have a canoe built in which they could sail far out on the ocean. The Chief went with his canoe-builders into the forest, so that they might mark for cutting down a large koa tree. They came to a great tree. But before they could put the ax to it two birds flew up to the very top of the tree and then cried out in a loud voice, "Say, Ke-awe, you cannot make a canoe out of this tree; it is hollow." And then they cried out, "A worthless canoe, a hollow canoe, a canoe that will never sail the ocean."

When the Chief heard this he turned from the tree, and he and his canoe-builders sought out another. They found another fine-looking tree, but before they put an ax to it, the same two birds flew up to the very top of it and cried out, "A worthless canoe, a hollow canoe, a canoe that will never sail the ocean." And to the top of every tree that the Chief and his canoe-builders thought was a good-timbered tree, the birds flew and made their unlucky cry, "A worthless canoe, a hollow canoe, a canoe that will never sail the ocean."

Day after day the Chief and his canoe-makers went into the forest, and day after day the birds flew to the top of every tree that they would cut down. At last the Chief saw that he could get no canoe-making tree out of the forest until he had killed the birds that made the unlucky cry.

So he sent for Prince Mai-ne-le to have him kill the birds while they were crying on the tree top. And he promised him, or anyone else who would kill the birds, his daughter in marriage and a part of the land of his kingdom.

Now when the sisters heard of the Chief's offer they made up their minds that the boy who had come to them should win the Chief's daughter and a portion of the land of the island. So they went to where Pi-ko-i was, and he told him all that they had heard. "And if you are able to shoot birds as you are able to shoot rats," they said, "you will become son-in-law to the Chief and one of the great men of the island. But Prince Mai-ne-le is going to let fly his arrow at the birds, and perhaps you will not want to match yourself with him," said they.

When his sisters said that, Pi-ko-i rose up from where he was sitting, and he said: "I am going to shoot at the birds that make the unlucky cry, and you must do this for me." Thereupon he told the women that they should make a large basket, and that they should tell everyone that this basket was for the safekeeping of their idol. Into this basket he, Pi-ko-i, would go and remain hidden there. And his sisters were to go with Prince Mai-ne-le's party, and they were to bring the basket with them, being careful, though, to let no one find out that there was a man in the basket. The women made the basket out of i-e vines, and Pi-ko-i went and hid in it. Then they took the great basket, and went and joined Mai-ne-le's party.

The canoes made swift passage, for the evening breeze behind them sent them flying, and by the dawn of the next morning they were able to make out the waterfalls on the steep cliffs of the land where the forest was that the Chief walked in. They landed. The sisters were able to get men to carry the basket that had, as all supposed, their idol in it. They entered the forest, and they came to where the Chief and his canoe-makers were.

They were under a great koa tree. To mark it the men raised their axes. As they did so the birds flew to the top of it and cried out their unlucky cry: "Say, Ke-awe, you cannot make a canoe out of this tree. A worthless canoe, a hollow canoe, a canoe that will never sail the ocean!"

As soon as the cry was heard Prince Mai-ne-le shot at them. His arrow did not go anywhere near the birds, so high was the tree top, so far above were they. Then the Chief's men built a platform that was half the height of the tree. From the platform Mai-ne-le shot at the birds again, and again his arrow failed to reach them. Then Pi-ko-i from the basket whispered. "Ask Mai-ne-le and ask the Chief why the birds still cry out and why they have not been hit. Is it because Mai-ne-le is not really shooting at them?" His sisters said all this to the Chief. Prince Mai-ne-le, when he heard what was said, replied, "Why do you not shoot at the birds yourself?" And then he said: "There are the birds, and here is the weapon. Now see if you can hit them." "Well," said the women, "we will ask our idol." They opened the basket then, and Pi-ko-i appeared. He had changed so much since he had eaten the feast in his sisters' house that no one there knew him for the stranger boy who had beaten Mai-ne-le in the shooting match before.

And what he said made all of them amazed. He asked the Chief to have a gourd of water brought to the tree. It was brought. Pi-ko-i then stood looking into the water. He saw the reflection of the birds that were on the tree top far, far above. He held his arms above his head; his arrow was aimed at the birds whose reflection he saw in the water. He brought the arrow into line with them; he let it fly. It struck both of them; they fell; they came tumbling down. Into the gourd of water they fell, and the people, on seeing the great skill shown by Pi-ko-i, raised a great shout.

Then the canoe-makers got to work, and after many days' labor they hewed down the great tree. The canoe was built for the Chief and the Chieftainess, and they went in it and sailed on the ocean. Pi-ko-i was with them when they made the voyage. But before that, they had given him their daughter in marriage, and together with the girl they had given him a portion of the land of Hawaii. Out of the portion that was given him Pi-ko-i gave land to his sisters' husbands, and the men became rich. And as for Mai-ne-le, he was made so ashamed by his second defeat by young Pi-ko-i that he went straight back to his own land and never afterward did he shoot an arrow.

THE STORY OF MO-E MO-E

ALSO A STORY ABOUT PO-O AND ABOUT KAU-HU-HU THE SHARK-GOD, AND ABOUT MO-E MO-E'S SON, THE MAN WHO WAS BOLD IN HIS WISH

LIGHT it now. One ku-kui nut and then another will burn along the string as I tell my stories. It is well that you have brought so many nuts, my younger brother.

At Ke-kaa lived Ma-ui and Mo-e Mo-e; they were friends, but no two men could be more different: the great desire of one was to go traveling, doing mighty deeds, and the great desire of the other was to sleep. While Ma-ui would be traveling, Mo-e would be sleeping. He was called O-pe-le at first, but afterward he was called Mo-e Mo-e because no one before or since ever slept so much as he: he could keep asleep from the first day of the month to the last day of the month; if a thunderstorm happened, it would wake him up; if no thunderstorm happened, he might go on sleeping for a whole year.

Once he went off traveling. He had not gone far when he lay down by the roadway and slept. While he was sleeping a freshet of water flowed down and covered him with pebbles and brambles and grasses—covered all of him except his nostrils. Then a ku-kui nut rested in his nostril and began to grow. It grew tall; it began to tickle his nostril; and then Mo-e Mo-e wakened up. "Here am I," he said, "at my favorite pastime, sleeping, and yet I am wakened up by this cursed ku-kui tree." He started off then to find his friend Ma-ui.

He did not find Ma-ui. He found, however, a woman whom he liked, and he married her and settled down in her part of the country. His wife had much land, and Mo-e Mo-e went out and worked on it. He needed no more sleep for a while, and he worked night and day until all the lands that his wife owned were cleared and planted. Then one day he told her that he would have to return to his own country. "And if something should happen to prevent my coming back to you," said he to his wife, "and if a child should be born to us, name the child, if it should be a girl, for yourself; but if it should be a boy, name him Ka-le-lea." His wife said she would remember what he told her, and Mo-e Mo-e started off on his journey.

On his way he felt sleepy, and he lay down by the roadside. He fell into one of his long slumbers. He had been sleeping for ten days, or perhaps for two less than ten days, when two men came along, and, seeing him lying there, took him up and carried him on their backs to where their canoe was moored.

Now these were two men who had been sent out to find a man who might be sacrificed to one of the gods in the temple. They were highly pleased when they came upon one who could give them such little trouble. They put Mo-e Mo-e in their canoe and brought him to the Island of Kau-ai. He didn't waken all the time they were at sea. They carried him to the temple, and still he did not waken. Then they made ready to sacrifice him to the god who was there.

While they were waiting for the hour of the sacrifice, a thunderstorm came. That made Mo-e Mo-e wake up. He saw where he was: and the pig that was to be sacrificed, and the bananas, the fish, and the awa, were beside him. He saw the two men who had taken him, squatting down with a spear between them, and he heard what they were saying. They, like us here, were telling a story. "And so," said one, "Ka-ma-lo went on his way." Mo-e Mo-e listened, and he heard part of the story.

Ka-ma-lo, a squealing pig upon his shoulder (said the second man), went hurrying on his way.

No man going into danger ever went so quickly as Ka-ma-lo did. And he was going into great danger, for he was on his way to the cavern where the Shark-God Kau-hu-hu had his abode. And you know, my comrade, that if a man had ever ventured into that cavern before, he never came out of it alive.

He came to it. Before the cavern was the great sea. Inside of it were Mo-o and Waka, the Shark-God's watchmen.

When they saw a man hurrying up to the cavern with a squealing pig upon his shoulders, Waka and Mo-o shouted to him to go back. But Ka-ma-lo came right up to them. "Our lord is away," they said, "and it is lucky for you, O man, that he is away. Fly for your life, for he will soon return." Ka-ma-lo would not go. He put down on the ground the pig which he had brought.

Waka and Mo-o ran here and there, beseeching Ka-ma-lo to go away. The man would not go. "I have brought this pig as an offering to the Shark-God," he said, "and I will speak to him even if afterward he destroy me." "It is now too late for you to get away," said Waka, "for, lo, our lord returns." "Hide yourself in the cavern; tie up your pig, and perhaps when our lord sleeps you will be able to get away," said Mo-o. They tied the pig, and they covered it up with seaweed; Ka-ma-lo went into the cavern and hid behind one of the rocks.

A great rolling wave came to the cavern; another came, and then another. With the eighth roller the Shark-God came out of the ocean. Ka-ma-lo looked out and saw him. And when he looked upon him he trembled and drew himself farther into the depths of the cavern.

The Shark-God transformed himself. He was now in the shape of a man, but he was taller and broader than any two men that Ka-ma-lo had ever seen. He came within the cavern, and Ka-ma-lo saw that he had still one mark of the shark upon him: on his back and between his great shoulders there were, as if made with tatto, the lines of a shark's opened mouth.

When he came within, Kau-hu-hu began to sniff. "I smell a man, a man," he said. Ka-ma-lo quaked with terror: the Shark-God, with his great height and breadth, seemed fearful to the man.

And still he moved about the cavern, and Mo-o and Waka, his watchmen, ran this way and that way, striving to get him to give up his search. There was a squealing outside. Kau-hu-hu stopped and ordered his watchmen to bring to him the thing that squealed. They went outside and came back with Ka-ma-lo's pig.

"A pig!" sniffed the Shark-God. "Then there must be a man about. Where is he?"

Then, in their terror, the two watchmen pointed to where Ka-ma-lo had hidden himself. The Shark-God put down his two big hands and drew the man up.

"Man, I will eat you," said the Shark-God.

"I have brought this pig as an offering to you," said Ka-ma-lo. "Do not eat me."

Then Kau-hu-hu wondered at a man's being so bold as to come within his cavern with an offering for him. "Man, why have you come?" he said.

Then said Ka-ma-lo: "Kau-hu-hu, you are a shark, but you are also a god. I have come to ask you to avenge me upon a cruel King and a wicked people. No one else is able to exact the vengeance that my soul craves, and so I have come where no man ever ventured before—into your cavern and into your presence."

"I am a shark, but I am also a god," said Kau-hu-hu, "and if that King and that people deserve the vengeance that you crave, it shall be wrought upon them. But if they do not deserve that vengeance, I will kill you and devour you for having come into my cavern."

"I will tell you why I crave vengeance on that King and on

that people." And thereupon Ka-ma-lo told the Shark-God all that he had suffered.

The King of the land I live in (said Ka-ma-lo) is the owner of a drum, and it is a drum that he had brought to him from far Kahiki. He would not let anyone strike on this drum but himself. He made a place for the drum, a sacred inclosure that no one might go into. Now the King of my land, Ku-pa, is a cruel King; indeed, so cruel is he that his people have become cruel, for the kind and the gentle have fled away, and those who have remained under his rule have become harder and harder. And at last it has come about that no one will get angry at even the worst thing that the King will do.

I wish that I had fled from the land when others fled. But I had two children, boys, and there was no place that I might have taken them to. They used to play with the King's children. Yesterday I went into the forest to choose a tree that might be made into a new canoe, for I am the King's canoe-builder. And while I was away my two boys went toward the King's house. They came before the inclosure where the drum was kept. The King's children were not there to play with, and my two boys played with each other for a while.

Now and then they would stand before where the drum was placed, and look at it. They did not know that Ku-pa was watching them—watching to see what the children would do.

At last the boys went into the sacred inclosure and their going there broke the law that the King had made. They sat down there, my two sons, and they struck upon the drum. They could have struck upon it so that the whole land would hear, or they could have struck so softly that the noise would be only like the fall of rain upon leaves. And that was how they struck the drum; the noise that they made was only a little noise and like the falling of rain upon the leaves in the forest.

But the King heard even that little sound; he came very softly up to the inclosure. The boys looked around. They saw him standing there; his eyes were hard as I have seen them, and his lips were cruel and revengeful. He called for his executioner. The executioner came; he slew my two boys in the inclosure where the King's drum is kept.

All that happened while I was in the forest. When I came back I went into the inclosure where the King's canoes are sheltered. I stood there beside the great canoe that was painted red. I put my hands upon it, for then I greatly rejoiced in this work of my hands. I put my hands along the outrigger of the canoe. And then I looked down, and it seemed to me that I saw a hand stretched out from under the canoe.

I stooped down, and I looked under it. I saw two bodies with their hands outstretched. I drew them out, and I saw that they were the bodies of my sons. And when I looked upon them I knew that my sons had been slain by the King's executioner.

I went away from the King's house. I met many men, and I spoke to them, telling them of the terrible thing that the King had done to me. But each one I spoke to said: "Yes, such is Ku-pa, our King. He has not dealt with you harder than he has dealt with others." And when they said this they looked at me; and I saw that their looks were hard, even as the King's.

I went within my house, and I sat there thinking. To whom could I go for vengeance on the King? Who would be powerful enough to avenge me upon Ku-pa? And then I thought of you, Kau-hu-hu. You would be able to avenge me, and no one else would be able. And so I made up my mind to go to you—even to go into the cavern where no man had ever ventured before.

I took a pig as an offering, and I went hurrying on my way; no man going into danger ever went so swiftly before.

Mo-e Mo-e heard no more of the story then. He stood up. The

two who were guarding him were so startled that they did not lay hands on him. He took up the spear that was between them, and he went off.

Back to his wife's he went, and he left the long spear with its edge of shark's teeth in the house. "I will have to make another journey," he said, "and if again anything should happen to me that will prevent my coming back, and if a son is born to us, and if he should want to go in search of me, give him the spear so that I may know him; and give him the name that I told you."

He went to work in the fields again, and he worked day and night, and his wife's brother Po-po-lo-au and her servant Po-o were astonished at the work he did. And then, on the very night that his son was born, Mo-e Mo-e fell asleep. He slept for ten days and for another ten days. His wife, her brother, and her servant tried to waken him; all they could do could not waken Mo-e Mo-e. Then his wife shook him; she made noises; she poured water on his eyes, but still he slept. Then she said, "There is no doubt about it: Mo-e Mo-e is dead."

She called her brother and her servant, and she said to them: "The Chief is dead. Wrap him up and carry him to the beach and cast him into the sea; that is the best that one can do for a dead man." Her brother and her servant did as she ordered, and a wrap was put around Mo-e Mo-e, and then he was carried down to the beach and cast into the sea. Then Po-po-lo-au went home, and Po-o went home.

His wife's name was Ka-le-ko'o-ka-lau-ae, and concerning her and her brother Po-po-lo-au and her servant Po-o a strange story is told. After they had left what they thought was the dead body of Mo-e Mo-e in the sea, Po-po-lo-au and Po-o went up the mountains to get timbers for the roofing of a house. They were far from home, and the night came on dark and rainy. Po-o wanted to go back to the house, but Po-po-lo-au would not return through the dark and the rain. Nothing would do him but that they should spend the night in a cave.

So they went into a cave that no one had ever gone into before. And at Po-po-lo-au's desire they lighted a great fire to keep themselves from the cold. And then, although there were things in the cave that they should have been fearful about, they both went to sleep.

In the middle of the night Po-po-lo-au was startled by something that he thought was happening. He wakened up, and he saw that the fire was burning Po-o. He called him, but the servant would not waken up. He went to him and tried to rouse him, but still he would not awaken. The fire, which had been burning the man's feet, went farther up his body. Po-po-lo-au lifted him and tried by every way to bring him to wakefulness, but there was no stir from Po-o. Then, when the fire had burned up to his neck, Po-po-lo-au let him lie there and ran out of the cave. He ran toward a hill. When he reached the top of it he heard a voice calling to him, "Wait until I come to you, and we will go home together." He looked back, and he saw a head with fire streaming out of it coming up the hill after him.

He ran to the valley, and the head rolled down the hill after him. He looked back, and he saw tongues of fire shooting out of the rolling head, and he became more frightened than before. He ran on and on. Through many valleys he raced, and always the head raced behind him. He reached the plain, and then he could hardly go on because of the terror he was in.

It happened that at that time a wizard was walking with his friends along that plain. "Do you see the person who is coming toward us?" he said. "If he is not caught until he comes up to us, he will be saved. But if he is caught before that, I do not know what will happen to him." As he said that, Po-po-lo-au came running up to them; and then the head did not come any nearer.

Po-po-lo-au told the wizard all that had befallen him. Then he went to his sister, the wife of Mo-e Mo-e. She asked about her servant, and he told her of how he had been burned and how his head had chased him.

Then the wizard came into the house. "I have come to you," he said, "because I fear you may be burned. The head that chased this man will come here. It will want to come within and stay in the house, but do not ask it to come in, or you will come into its power. It will ask you to go outside to it, but do not go out. It will ask you to send your child out to it, but do not send him out."

And then he said: "When you hear a whistle outside, it will mean that the head is near. Then move into a corner of the house and keep very still. When the outside is all lighted up you will know that it has come, and when the inside is lighted up you will know that it has entered the house."

The woman stayed within the house, and about the middle of the night she heard a whistle outside; then all outside was lighted up, and the voice of Po-o called to her, asking her to come without. "I will not go outside, for it is raining," she said. "There is no rain," said the voice of Po-o.

Then the voice spoke again and said to her, "Send out to me your little child." And the voice went on to say: "I have what your child liked well—ripe bananas. Send him out to me, and I will give them to him."

"I will not send him out to you," the woman said, "for the child is now asleep."

Then the head came within the house, but the woman had hidden herself and was not to be found. The wizard stole in; he drew the woman out of the house, and he closed the door. The head called out: "Do not close the door on me; I wish to come outside." But those outside blocked up the door and would not let it out, for they knew that what was within the house was the demon of the cave that had gone into the man's head. Then fire burst out in the house; there were twelve loud sounds; the head was shattered, and after that there was nothing ever seen of it. And that is the strange story about Po-o.

And now we can speak of Mo-e Mo-e, or at least we can speak of Mo-e Mo-e's son. He grew up with a stepfather, for his mother had married again. Now, the stepfather was not always kind to Mo-e Mo-e's son, and the boy was often punished by him.

One day he said to his mother: "I will go in search of my real father." "Your father is dead and in the sea," said his mother. "Perhaps he is not," said the boy. "I will go in search of him, and I will bring with me the spear that my father left for me."

So he started off in search of Mo-e Mo-e, his father. Now when Mo-e Mo-e had been flung into the sea long before, he had gone down to the bottom. He lay there, for his slumber was still deep. The fish bit at him, but they did not awaken him, and the salt of the deep sea went into his skin. Still he lay there asleep. Then a thunderstorm came. He wakened up. He went to the surface of the sea. Then he swam to the shore.

He had been made bald by the salt water that had got into his skin. His skin had been scraped off by the bites of the fishes. He crawled to a pigpen, and there he lay down. From that place he crawled to another place. There a wizard found him; he gave Mo-e Mo-e medicine that cured him.

Then he went back to his own home, to the place that he had first come from. He went on no more trips after that, and he took to sleeping like an ordinary man.

And now his son, with the great spear of dark red wood with the ridges of shark's teeth upon it, went off in search of him. He came to the island where Mo-e Mo-e had lived when his name was O-pe-le. He went down into the valley where O-pe-le had had his farm.

The boy came to a field where a man was planting taro. He

sat down to watch the man, holding the spear in his hands. Two
men came along. Seeing the spear that the boy held, they
stopped and looked at it. "Is it not like the spear we carried when
we took away the man who slept all the way in our canoe and all
the time on the black stones of the temple?" one said to the
other. "It is the very same spear," said the other. "You laid it
down, and I was looking at it while I was telling you the story
of Ka-ma-lo, who went to the cave of the Shark-God." "I never
heard the rest of that story," said the first man, "and I should
like to hear it."

The two sat together, and then the man who had been telling
the story that Mo-e Mo-e had heard, went on.

When Ka-ma-lo had told him all that had happened, the
Shark-God said to him: "Go back to Ku-pa's country and live
there with his people. But make ready a great offering for me—
an offering of black pigs, white fowl, and red fish—and when
the new moon comes take the offering into the temple inclosure,
and stay there until you see a cloud coming over the mountains
of La-na-i. And when you see that cloud, leave the temple inclosure and get into your canoe and go out to sea." So Kau-hu-
hu said; then he lay down in the cavern and went to sleep. Ka-
ma-lo did not stay any longer; he went quickly out of the
cavern.

He went back, and he lived for a while under the cruel King
who had destroyed his children and amongst the hard people
that the King ruled over. He began to put together the offering
for Kau-hu-hu the Shark-God; and by the time he had got all
the black pigs and all the white fowl and all the red fish, the
new moon had come.

He took his offering to the temple inclosure; he left the black
pigs and the white fowl and the red fish within, and he stood
upon the black stones, and he looked toward the mountains of
La-na-i.

He heard the King beating upon his drum: it was to sum-
mon all his people to him. He heard the sound of the drum, but
he did not go toward the King's house; he stood upon the black
stones that made the temple inclosure, and he watched and he
waited, moveless as the stone that he stood on. Louder and
louder beat the King's drum. The people all gathered at his
house. Then Ka-ma-lo saw a speck of cloud over the mountains
of La-na-i. He watched, and he saw it coming nearer and nearer.
He left the place that he had been watching from, and he went
to the beach.

As he went he saw the crowd of people that were gathered
together by the King's drum. They called to him, but he went
past them. He came to the beach, and he pushed out in his canoe.

When he looked back he saw that the end of the rainbow was
now resting on the temple inclosure, and he knew that the
Shark-God had set a guard on the offering that he had left there.
The cloud was coming nearer, and it was growing bigger and
bigger as it came. It made a darkness over all the land.

Ka-ma-lo paddled beyond the reef, and he went far out to
sea. Out of the darkness that covered the land there came a
fearful storm: down poured the rain; the trees in the forest
cracked and broke; the rivers suddenly filled up; as they rushed
into the valley, trees, houses, and men were swept away and out
to sea. Ka-ma-lo, in his canoe, saw the red-covered drum of the
King go floating by. That was the end of Ku-pa and his people.
And if the spear that this young man holds in his hands be the
same spear that I had when we were in the temple inclosure the
day I told you the beginning of the story, that spear is the only
thing that has come out of his kingdom.

Ka-le-lea then spoke up and said: "Yes, this is the spear you
carried on that occasion, for my father, Mo-e Mo-e, heard you
tell the beginning of that story; he related it to my mother, who
told it to me. And now I am seeking him; I am seeking that man,

for he is my father." "If you are seeking the man who slept while we brought him to the temple and slept there while we were making the preparations to sacrifice him, you have not far to go," said the men. "We have seen him since, and we know where he is." "And where is he?" asked the boy. "The man planting taro there," said the man, "is no other than he; he is O-pe-le, who came to be called Mo-e Mo-e."

Then the boy called out to the man who was planting taro in the field, "Say, your rows of taro are crooked." The man looked at his rows, and then he began to straighten them. But no matter how he straightened them, the boy would call out the same thing. Then the man said to himself: "How strange this is! Here I have been doing this work night and day, and my rows were never made crooked before. Now it seems that I cannot make them straight." Thereupon he quit working and went to the edge of the patch where the boy was standing, the great spear in his hands. "Whose offspring are you?" said he, when he looked at the boy and looked at the spear. "Yours," said the boy, "yours and Ka-le-ko'o-ka-lau-ae's." "What name have you?" said the man. "I am Ka-le-lea," said the boy. "You have found me, my son," said Mo-e Mo-e.

And thereupon the two went into the house.

The boy who came to Mo-e Mo-e, Ka-le-lea, is also known in our stories; in them he is called "The Man Who Was Bold in His Wish," and when you have lighted some more ku-kui nuts I will tell you how he came to get that name.

When he grew up he became a fisherman, and he and another youth had a house together. Ke-ino was the other youth's name. Now whenever other houses were dark, Ka-le-lea and Ke-ino's would be lighted up. They would have gathered many ku-kui nuts, they would string them together, and they would light them up. And the light that Ka-le-lea and Ke-ino had in their house would be seen by travelers and watchmen and those who looked out of their houses at night. What was being done in the house where there was so much light? people wondered.

Well, when Ka-le-lea and Ke-ino came into their house in the evening, they would, first of all, partake of their evening meal. Then they would light the ku-kui nuts and keep lighting them as they burned out. Then they would lie down on their mats with their pillows under their heads, and they would look up at the roof, Ka-le-lea looking at the gable end, and Ke-ino looking at the end opposite. They would watch the mice running along the ridgepole of the house. Then one would say to the other: "Here are we, Ka-le-lea and Ke-ino, awake and with lights burning beside us. Let us keep watching the mice running along the ridgepole of our house, and as we watch them, let each of us tell out his wishes."

Then Ke-ino would say: "Here is my wish. I wish that we may sleep until the first crowing of the cock, then waken up, and go into the field and pull up a root for fish bait. Then go down to the beach, pound the root and set it for eel bait. Then catch an eel after having waited around the beach for a bit, go home with it, and wrap it in banana leaves for cooking. Put it in the oven after a while. Then, at the second crowing of the cock, open the oven and put the eel one side to cool. Eat, after a while, until we have had enough. Then lie down on our mats, put the pillows under our heads, look up and watch the mice run along the ridgepole of our house, and tell out our wishes. That is my wish, brother."

Then Ka-le-lea would say: "It is a wish, but it is not a manly wish. Listen now, and I will tell out my wishes.

"I wish that we may eat King Ka-ku-hi-hewa's dogs that bite the faces of the people. I wish that we may eat his hogs with the crossing tusks. I wish that we may eat the fat fish of his ponds. And when we have eaten all belonging to him, I wish that the

King himself may prepare the drink for us, bring it to us, and put his own cup to our lips. And then, when we have eaten and drunken, I wish that the King may send for his two daughters, have them brought in, and have each of them marry one of us, and then have each couple go to live in a house that he has had built for them. That is my wish, my brother, and I want you to know it."

But when Ka-le-lea would say this (and he would say it every night) Ke-ino would pull the mat over his face, and he would say: "No, not that wish. Never let it pass your lips again. We will surely get killed on account of that wish."

Now the King whom Ka-le-lea had spoken of was at that time engaged in a war—the war of King Ka-ku-hi-hewa against King Pueo-nui. He had won nothing so far in the war, and he was becoming disheartened. His watchmen and his soldiers often saw the light in the house of Ka-le-lea and Ke-ino, and one day they told the King about it.

Then the King sent his spy to see or hear what was going on in that house. The spy stole up and lay outside. He heard Ke-ino tell his wish, and then he heard Ka-le-lea tell his. He heard nothing more; before the first cock crew he stole away, leaving his dagger stuck at the entrance of the house to let Ka-le-lea and Ke-ino know that the King's servant had been there.

When the spy came back to the King's house, the King was there with his Councilor beside him, and they were talking about what should be done to bring to some sort of end the war against King Pueo-nui. Said the King when the spy came to them: "What is happening in the house that I sent you to?"

Said the spy: "This and this." Thereupon he told all he had heard. When he spoke about Ka-le-lea's wish the King became very angry. "Because I am not winning the war," he said, "these people think they can make mock of me! Eat my dogs and my hogs and my fat fish indeed! Have me prepare the drink for them and put my own cup to their mouths! And then give my

daughters in marriage to two such fellows!.Tell me, my Councilor, how should I have them slain?"

But the Councilor was not for having Ka-le-lea and Ke-ino
put to death in any way. "Rather carry out the wish that the
boldest of them spoke out," he said. "If anyone can help you in
the war, it is that man. Send for both of them and carry out the
bold one's wish to the very end. You have a wish too: it is to
win the whole island for yourself. That man, believe me, is the
one who can help you to have that wish of yours made real."
The King agreed at last to let Ka-le-lea and Ke-ino live, and
he even agreed to carry out to its very end the wish that Ka-le-
lea had made. He ordered his men to cut timber and build
houses for the two fishermen and the wives he was going to give
them, and after that he sent an officer with soldiers to bring
Ka-le-lea and Ke-ino to him.

Ke-ino was the first to waken up that morning. And when he
went to the door he saw the dagger that was stuck at the entrance. Then he knew that the King's servant had been listening
in the night and that he had heard all that had been said. "We
are going to be killed," he said to Ka-le-lea; "your terrible wish
has been overheard, and the two of us are going to die for it."

But Ka-le-lea only stirred on the mat he was lying on; he
didn't even get up to go to the door. And then Ke-ino saw a
company of people coming out of the King's house. They carried
axes. "Here are our deaths," said Ke-ino. But the procession he
saw was that of the King's servants as they went toward the
mountain to cut timbers for the two houses that were to be built,
according to the Councilor's advice and the King's orders, for
himself and Ka-le-lea and the wives who were to be given to
them—the King's two daughters.

Later on, another procession came from the King's house.
This one came straight toward their house. The men were armed
with spears, and the officers had on their shoulders cloaks of

bright feathers, and their war helmets were on their heads. Ke-ino said: "Our deaths are now close to us." But all that Ka-le-lea answered was: "Keep your eye on them."

He did not move until then. Then he rose up from the mat he had been sleeping on, and he took up his club. He went outside, and by this time the armed men had come up. The officer said: "We have come to take you two before the King." Ka-le-lea said never a word, but with his great club he struck the house a mighty blow, and he scattered its thatch and its timbers in all directions.

Then, very much to their surprise, Ka-le-lea and Ke-ino were put into a litter and carried on the shoulders of the soldiers. They were brought before the King. They were served according to the wish of Ka-le-lea: the dogs and the hogs and the fat fish were given them to eat; the King prepared the drink for them, and in his own cup he brought it to Ka-le-lea and Ke-ino. And when they had drunken, the King's daughters were brought before them. One was wed to Ka-le-lea, and the other was wed to Ke-ino. And then each couple was given a house to live in, a house that the King had had built for them in a single day.

Ka-le-lea, the one who had uttered the bold wish, was not seen much after that. He stayed in the house that had been given him. Ke-ino was the one who was around all the time. And the King took Ke-ino and made him an officer, and gave him a feather cape for his shoulders and a war helmet to go on his head. After that, Ke-ino went into the fight with a company of men; every day he won a victory. But, for all that, the war still went on.

Ka-le-lea stayed in the house all day with his wife, the King's daughter. He had no war helmet, no feather cape, and he never took a company of men out to battle. Ke-ino was the great man now, and Ka-le-lea was never spoken of.

Still the war went on. But after the first crow of the cock, a man with a great club used to go to Ha-la-wa, where the officers and chiefs of Pueo-nui's army were, and do battle with them. This the man did every day. He would come upon a company of them, and fight with them, striking right and left with his club. He would slay them all. Then he would gather up their feather capes and their war helmets, and he would run, run away. The fighting chiefs were all killed by him, and Pueo-nui's army melted away. There were stories about how the chiefs were killed in the early morning, and of how their feather capes and their war helmets were taken away. No one knew the warrior who fought with them and overcame them. But the King was sure that Ke-ino was the one who did it all.

When the last of Pueo-nui's fighting chiefs was killed, an end came to the war, and Pueo-nui gave his lands and his kingdom to King Ka-ku-hi-hewa. And that very morning, as the stranger warrior who had done battle with the chiefs was running back, he was seen by a watchman in the light of the early morning. The watchman flung a spear at the running man. It struck him on the arm, just above the wrist. He kept on running. The spear had a hook, and the watchman knew that it would be hard for the warrior to draw it out of the flesh of his arm.

And now the King made up his mind to give a great reward to Ke-ino, and to get rid of Ka-le-lea, the fellow whom no one had ever seen outside his house. He made a proclamation, declaring his victory in the war, and telling how much of it was due to his son-in-law Ke-ino. And everyone was satisfied, for everyone was sure that Ke-ino had won the war. Everyone, that is, except the King's Councilor and the watchman who had flung the spear at the running man. The watchman kept on saying that it was not Ke-ino but another man who had slain the fighting chiefs of Pueo-nui's army and had carried off their feather capes and their war helmets.

The Councilor advised the King to bring all his people together, men women, and children. All came to a place near the

King's house—all but those who fell down and who were not able to get up again. "Are all your people here, O King?" asked the Councilor. "All are here," said the King, "except that fellow Ka-le-lea. He is asleep at home. His father, they say, was a good sleeper, and my son-in-law takes after his father." "Nevertheless," said the Councilor, "send for him, and bring him here."

Then Ka-le-lea was sent for. He came, and he saw all the people gathered before the King's house. He saw Ke-ino there in great state, with a bright feather cape on his shoulders and a war helmet on his head. He looked at Ke-ino, and Ke-ino looked at him. The watchman, who had been looking at all who came, saw him, and he made a sign to the Councilor.

Then said the Councilor to the King: "Send to this man's house, and have a search made in it. And all that your men find hidden in it, have them bring here." Men were sent to Ka-le-lea's house. They returned with feather capes and war helmets enough to make a great pile. And then the watchman pointed to Ka-le-lea's arm, and showed the hook of a spear in the flesh of it.

And when the watchman told of how he had flung his spear at the warrior who had slain the last of Pueo-nui's fighting chiefs, it was seen by all that Ka-le-lea, and not Ke-ino, was the man who had won the war. After that he was made the King's chief officer. But he did nothing against Ke-ino, who came to serve under him.

And this is the story of Mo-e's son, Ka-le-lea. Soon after, Ka-ku-hi-hiwa died. Ka-le-lea came to rule in his stead, for all the people clamored to have over them *The Man Who Was Bold in His Wish.*

THE STORY OF
HA-LE-MA-NO

AND THE PRINCESS KAMA

IN Puna lived the Princess Kama, and she was so beautiful
that two Kings strove to win her—the King of Puna and the
King of Hilo. They sent presents to her mother and to her
father and to herself. But Kama never saw either of those Kings.
She was sent to live in a house that no one was permitted to
enter except herself and her brother. "In a while Kama will
come to the height of her beauty," her parents said, "and then
we will give her to be Queen to one of these Kings. But until
that time comes no one must speak to her." And so, in a house
that was forbidden to everyone else, Kama lived with only her
young brother for her companion.

Far away, on the Island of Oahu, there lived a youth whose
name was Ha-le-ma-no. Every night he had a dream in which
he met a beautiful maiden who talked to him and whose name
in his dream he knew. But when he wakened up he could not
remember what name she had told him to call her by, nor what
words they had said to each other. He remembered only her
beautiful form and face, the dress and the wreaths she wore, and
the scent that was in her dress. The youth became so that he

could think of nothing else except this maiden, and he wasted away because of this thought that put every other thought out of his mind. Then it came about that he would eat no food, and at last his fasting and his wasting thought brought him near his death.

But Ha-le-ma-no had a sister who had magical powers. Her name was Lae-ni-hi. She was traveling with her other sisters when she saw Ha-le-ma-no's image in the sky, and she knew by that sign that her brother was near his death. Her sisters wept for Ha-le-ma-no when they saw that sign in the sky, but Lae-ni-hi uttered a magic spell, and through that spell Ha-le-ma-no was brought back to life.

Then she went and she visited her brother, and when she was with him she asked what it was that had brought him so near his death. "It is because of a maiden whom I dream of continually," he told her, "that I was near my death, and that I may come near my death again."

His sister asked him what the maiden was like, and he told her. "She is tall and very beautiful, and she seems to be a Princess. She has a wreath of hala on her head and a lei of lehua blossoms around her neck. Her dress is of scented tapa, and it is dyed red." "It is in Puna," said his sister, "that the women wear the lehua lei, and have scented tapa for their dresses."

Then she asked, "How do your meetings come about?" "When I fall asleep," said Ha-le-ma-no, "the maiden comes to me. Then she tells me her name. But when I waken up I do not know the name I called her by."

He slept, and his wise sister watched over him. In his sleep he again met the beautiful maiden. She heard him speak the dream woman's name. It was Kama. Soon afterward Ha-le-ma-no wakened from his sleep.

"She is Kama, and of her I have heard much," said his sister.

"She is very beautiful. But no one is permitted to come into the house where she lives. And in a while, when she has reached the height of her beauty, she will be given in marriage to the King of Puna or the King of Hilo." "Unless I can take her out of that forbidden house and away from these two Kings," said Ha-le-ma-no, "I shall surely die."

Then his sister promised him that she would strive to find some way of bringing him and Kama together. He ate his food because she made that promise, and he became well again. Then, that he might be able to follow her travels, she told him of the signs she would show. "If it rains here," she said, "you will know that I have got as far as the Island of Mo-lo-kai. If the lightning flashes, you will know that I have reached the Island of Maui. If it thunders, I am at Kohala. And if you see red water flowing, I have reached Puna, where your Princess lives."

Ha-le-ma-no's sister started off. Soon it rained; soon the lightning flashed; soon thunder was heard; soon red water flowed. Lae-ni-hi had come to Puna.

When she came there she began to devise ways by which she could come to the Princess in her forbidden house. She caused the wind to blow. It aroused the sea from its repose, and the surf began to roll in on the beach of Kai-mu. That was a place where the people used to go for surf riding. When they saw the surf coming in in great rollers they began to shout. They got their surfboards and prepared to ride in on the rolling surf.

When Kama's brother heard the shouting he came down on the beach. He saw the people riding the surf, and he went back to ask his sister's permission to ride the surf like the others. She came down to the beach with him. And when she saw the surf coming in in such fine rollers she too became excited, and she longed to go riding it.

She allowed the first roller to come in until it reached the shore; she allowed the second roller to come in; then the third.

And when that roller reached the shore she plunged in and swam out with her board to the place where the rollers began to curve up. When she reached that place she took the first roller that came along, and, standing on her surfboard, she rode in on it. The people watching shouted in admiration for her, so beautiful was her figure as she stood upon the board that came racing in with the rolling surf.

She rode the surf three times, and she was becoming more and more delighted with the sport, when the wind ceased to blow and the surf went down. Kama was left in shallow water. She looked down, and she saw a bright fish in the water. And her brother, who was looking toward her, saw the fish at the same time. He called out to her, "O my sister, take up and bring to me the bright fish that is in the shallow water."

Now the fish was Lae-ni-hi, who had transformed herself. Kama put her hands under her and took her up. She put the fish into a calabash of water and gave her to her brother for a plaything. He carried the fish with him, and in that way Lae-ni-hi came into the house that was forbidden to all except the Princess and her brother.

In the middle of the night she changed back into a woman, and she stood above where the Princess lay. Kama wakened up and saw the stranger woman near her. "Where are you from?" the Princess asked. "I am from near here." "There is no woman who is like you anywhere near. Besides, no one belonging to this place would come into this house, for all know that it is forbidden." "I have come from beyond the sea." "Yes, now you are telling me the truth."

Then Lae-ni-hi asked the Princess if she had ever met a youth in her dream. The Princess would not answer when she asked this. "If you would have me bring one to you, give me a wreath that you have worn, and a dress," said Ha-le-ma-no's sister. Kama gave her a wreath that was withered and one of her scented dresses.

Lae-ni-hi went back to her brother. She showed him the wreath and the dress that the Princess had worn. Upon seeing these things Ha-le-ma-no was sure that his sister had been with the dream maiden, and he rose up to go at once to where she was.

But his sister would not let him go without her. And before she would go back to Puna she had toys and playthings made—toys and playthings that would take the fancy of Kama's young brother. She had wooden birds made that would float on the waves; she had a toy canoe made and painted red; in it there were men in red to paddle it; she had other figures made that could stand upright; then she fixed up a colored and high-flying kite.

With the toys and playthings in their canoe, Ha-le-ma-no and Lae-ni-hi started off for Puna. And when they drew near the shore Ha-le-ma-no let the kite rise up. As it went up in the air the people on the beach saw it, and they shouted. The Princess' brother heard the shouts, and he came out to see what was happening.

When he saw the kite he ran down to the beach. He saw a canoe with two persons in it, and one of them held the string of the kite. He called out to them, "Oh, let me have the thing that flies!" Lae-ni-hi then said to her brother, "Let the boy have it," and he put the string of the kite into the boy's hand. Then the birds were put into the water, and they floated on the waves. Then the toy canoe with its men in red was let down, and it floated on the water. The boy cried out, "Oh, let me have these things," and Lae-ni-hi gave them to him.

And then she put along the side of the canoe the standing figures that she had brought. The boy saw them, and them he wanted too. Then Lae-ni-hi said to him, "Are you a favorite with your sister?" "I am," the boy said; "she will do anything I ask her to do." "Call her so that she comes near us, and I will give you these figures." The boy then called her. "Unless you come here, sister," he said, "I cannot get these playthings."

Kama came near. Then Ha-le-ma-no saw that she had the very height of the maiden whom he had seen in his dreams. "Are you a favorite with your sister, and would she mind if you asked her to turn her back to us?" Lae-ni-hi said. The boy asked his sister to turn her back, and then Ha-le-ma-no saw how straight her back was. After this Lae-ni-hi said, "Are you a favorite with your sister, and would she mind if you asked her to show her face to us?" After that Kama stood facing the canoe, and Ha-le-ma-no saw that this was indeed the maiden of his dream.

Then they met, Ha-le-ma-no and Kama. The Princess knew him for the youth she had seen in her dreams. She let him take her by the hands and bring her into the canoe. When they were in the canoe Lae-ni-hi paddled it off. The people of Puna and the people of Hilo came in chase of them. But by the power that Lae-ni-hi had, the canoe was made to go so swiftly that those who followed were left far behind.

After this the two Kings said to each other: "Yes, we have sent much of what we owned to her and to her parents with the idea that one or the other of us would get her for his wife. Now she has been carried off from us. Let us make war upon those who have taken her, and punish them for having carried her off."

And so the two Kings made war upon Ha-le-ma-no's people. Ha-le-ma-no and Kama had to flee away. And after enduring much suffering and much poverty they came to the Island of Maui. There they lived; but instead of living in state and having plenty, they had to dig the ground and live as a farmer and a farmer's wife.

Near where they lived there was a beach, and people used to go down to it for surf riding. One day Kama went down to this beach. She took a board and went surf riding. And when she was racing in on the surf she remembered how she had once lived as a princess, and she remembered how Ha-le-ma-no had come and had taken her away, and how she had nothing now but a grass hut and the roots that she and her husband pulled out of the ground. And then she was angry with Ha-le-ma-no, and she longed to be back again in Puna.

When she finished surf riding and came in on to the shore she saw that there were red canoes there—the canoes of a king. And then she saw Hua-a, the King of Puna. He came to her, and he took her by the hands. She went with him, leaving her husband, who was working in his fields. But in a while she was sorry for what she had done, and she left Hua-a. And after that Kama went wandering through the islands.

Now when Ha-le-ma-no knew that his wife had left him, he grew so ill that again he was near his death. But again his sister saved him. Then, when he was well, Ha-le-ma-no told his sister that he would learn to be a fisherman, for he thought that if he were something else than a farmer Kama would come back to him.

His sister told him to learn to be a chanter of verses; she told him that, if he had that art, he would be most likely to win his wife back to him. Ha-le-ma-no made up his mind to learn the art of chanting verses.

When he was on his way to learn this art he passed by a grove at Ke-a-kui. He went within the grove, and he saw the mai-le vine growing on the ohia trees. Then he began to strip the vine from the trees and make wreaths of it. He was sitting down making the wreaths when he saw the top of the mountain Ha-le-a-ka-la, like a pointed cloud in the evening, with other clouds drifting about it. And when he looked upon that mountain he thought of the places where he and his wife had traveled. And as he was thinking of her, his wife, who had been wandering about that island, came near where he was. She saw him and she

knew him; she came and she stood behind him. And then Ha-
le-ma-no, looking upon the mountain, was moved to chant these
verses:

"I was once thought a good deal of, O my love!
My companion of the shady trees.
For we two once lived on the food from the long-speared grass
    of the wilderness.
Alas, O my love!
My love from the land of the Kau-mu-ku wind,
As it comes gliding over the ocean,
As it covers the waves of Papa-wai,
For it was the canoe that brought us here.
Alas, O my love!
My love of the home where we were friendless,
Our only friend being our love for one another.
It is hooked, and it bites to the very inside of the bones."

Kama was going to put out her hand to touch him, but, hearing
him chant this, she thought that he was in such sorrow that he
would never forgive her. She wept and she went away, leaving
the place without speaking to him.

After that Ha-le-ma-no went on his way; he learned the art
of chanting verses. Afterward, when he was very famous, it
happened that he was invited to a place where there were games
and chanting.

He came to that place; covered over with a mantle, he sat by
himself, and he watched those who came in. Many people came
in, and amongst them a woman who wanted to be a wife to Ha-
le-ma-no—a woman of great riches. But as Ha-le-ma-no looked
toward this woman, he saw sitting there, in all her beauty and
her grace, his own wife Kama. They asked him to chant to them.
Then he remembered how he and she had lived together and had

wandered together in different places; and, remembering this, he chanted:

"We once lived in Hilo, in our own home,
For we had suffered in the home that was not ours,
For I had but one friend, myself.
The streams of Hilo are innumerable,
The high cliff was the home where we lived.
Alas, my love of the lehua blossoms of Moku-pa-ne!
The lehua blossoms that were braided with the hala blossoms,
For our love for one another was all that we had.
The rain fell only at Le-le-wi,
As it came creeping over the hala trees at Po-mai-kai,
At the place where I was punished through love.
Alas, O my love!
My love from the leaping cliffs of Pi-i-kea;
From the waters of Wai-lu-ku where the people are carried
    under,
Which we had to go through to get to the many cliffs of Hilo,
Those solemn cliffs that are bare of people,
Peopled by you and me alone, my love,
You, my own love!"

And when she heard these verses Kama knew who the man was who chanted them. She bowed her head, and she chanted:

"Alas, thou art my bosom companion, my love!
My companion of the cold watery home of Hilo.
I am from Hilo,
From the rain that pelts the leaves of the breadfruit of Pi-i-
    honua;
For we live at the breadfruit trees of Malama.
Love is shown by the tears,
Love is the friend of my companion,

My companion of the thick forests of Pana-ewa,
Where you and I have trod,
Our only fellow traveler our love.
Alas, O my companion, my love!
My love of the cold, watery home of Hilo,
The friendless home where you and I lived."

And when she had chanted this, Kama looked toward Ha-le-ma-no, and she saw that forgiveness was in his eyes. They stood up then, and they joined each other. Then they went away together.

"You will surely see Hai-li,
Hai-li where the blossoming lehua trees
Are haunted by the birds,
The o-o of the forest,
Whose sweet notes can be heard at eventide."

So they chanted as they went away together.

"COMPANION-IN-SUFFERING-IN-THE-GLADE"

WHEN she was born she was left with the taro buds and the crushed sugarcanes, for no one would rear her as a child. Then her grandmother had a dream; in her dream a beautiful girl stood before her. "What do you want with me, beautiful one?" the grandmother said; "I have never looked upon you before." "I am the youngest daughter of your youngest daughter, and I want you to come for me." "And where shall I find you?" "You will find me amongst the taro buds and the crushed sugarcanes where the trash has been thrown out."

So the grandmother arose and hastened to the place where her youngest daughter lived. When she came near the place she saw a rainbow. Then her eyes became dim, and when she saw the rainbow again it was over the place where the trash had been thrown. She saw a child lying there with the crushed sugarcanes around it; she took the child up, wrapped it in a fold of her skirt, and took it to her home.

In twenty days it had become a beautiful girlchild—a girl whom her grandmother reared carefully until she was twenty years old. At that age she was like the beautiful girl who had appeared in her grandmother's dream; her figure was erect and faultless; her skin was firm and smooth like the covering of the young banana shoot, and her eyes were dark and soft like wela-weka. I do not know what name was given her then; I only know the name that was given her afterward; perhaps because she gathered the lehua blossoms and twined them into wreaths, she was called Lei-lehua.

Where she lived no one ever saw her except her grandmother and her attendant—no one else, neither man nor woman. And she saw no one else, neither woman nor man. And she never went from her grandmother's except to go into the forest to make her wreaths of lehua blossoms.

One day when she was in the forest with her attendant, the bird Elepaio appeared and called out to her from amongst the leaves. The notes that Elepaio made became words in her mind:

"Wend to Wai-a-hao, wend;
The fish is fine and the fruit."

Lei-lehua said to her attendant, "Is it a bird that is calling like that?" Her attendant said, "It may be a branch scratching against a branch, or it may be the wind going amongst the leaves." "Hark," said Lei-lehua. And again the notes of Elepaio made words in her mind:

"Wend to Wai-a-hao, wend;
The fish is fine and the fruit."

"There," said Lei-lehua, "I told you it was a bird."

Then the bird sang to them, and the notes that the bird made became words in Lei-lehua's breast.

> "This is the glade Haili,
> Where birds the lehua buds sip.
> What of the dells of Hilo
> Where awa upon the tree grows,
> And birds cry gathering the awa?"

When Elepaio cried this out, her attendant said to Lei-lehua, "Let us return home, for the time for stringing our wreaths of lehua has ended."

But as she said this, the notes of Elepaio sounded again, and in Lei-lehua's breast the notes became words:

> "Ye mists,
> Ye mists that creep in the uplands,
> Ye mists that creep toward the sea,
> Come, gather!"

And as the bird cried out this the mists came down and the mists gathered, and Lei-lehua and her attendant were lost to each other in the glade.

Still she heard the calling of the bird Elepaio. She followed the notes as they sounded, going away from where the trees grew. Then the mists lifted; the sun was setting, darkness was coming on, and there was a house before her.

She went within the house. There was a handsome youth there, and he greeted her. She greeted him, speaking in a low voice. Outside the bird Elepaio cried, telling the youth how he had found the girl in the glade of the lehua trees.

The youth was Ka-lama-ula, the son of a prince. He went to Lei-lehua and took her hands, and told her that he would have her stay with him as his wife. The maiden said to him: "O my lord, let me be! I am friendless, but let me remain for thirty

days, and then, perhaps, response to you will rise within me."
When she said this, more and more admiration grew in Ka-
lama-ula for the beautiful girl that the bird Elepaio had
brought him.

She stayed with the mother and with the sister of Ka-lama-
ula. In the night after the third day she was there, she had a
dream. In her dream a man came close to her; he was not like
Ka-lama-ula, the only man she had ever seen; this man had a
high feather helmet upon his head; on his shoulders there was
a cape of bright feathers, and he held in his hands a war club.
The man said to her: "Your grandmother promised that you
were to be mine. I have waited many days, and the spirit within
me has fainted because the promise given me has not been ful-
filled." "What must I do?" Lei-lehua said to him in her dream.
"You must prepare yourself to go on a strange journey." Lei-
lehua replied, "I did not come here with the consent of my
people, and the steps that led me here were not foreseen; therefore, I will take your words as a mantle to keep upon my
shoulders at all times."

When she woke up and knew that she had been dreaming, she
tried to fathom what she had dreamt, but she could not fathom
it. Her mind was possessed by a sense of a forest—that was all
that remained to her of her dream.

The next night the dream came to her again. The man whom
she now knew to be in the guise of a warrior came to her. Again
he told her of the promise that her grandmother had made him,
and again he spoke to her about preparing herself for a strange
journey. And in the morning she had a dream that she could not
fathom, and a sense of the forest possessed her.

She fell in love with the one who had come to her twice in
dream. But she could not come to him, so she folded her arms
and wept. When the youth Ka-lama-ula saw her weeping he
said, "Quiet yourself; not until many days have passed will you
have to tell me whether you have a love that responds to mine
or not." Lei-lehua made no answer to him. On the third night

she dreamt again of the man in the guise of a warrior; then, before dawn, she rose up and she left the house. She was ready now for the strange journey that the warrior in her dream had told her of.

When she had gone a little way the mountain clouds began to thicken; drops of rain began to fall one by one; the wind began to rise: then the mists crept over the ground, and a rainbow appeared and stayed before her. Again she was closed around with the mists, and all things were hidden from her view.

She went on. The mists lifted, and she went over the empty hills and across the empty plains, and she came into the uplands of Pu-hula-moa, a place altogether without people. There she lived. She spent her days in the glades gathering lehua blossoms and stringing them into wreaths. She tasted no food. When she slept the man in the guise of a warrior appeared to her in her dream.

Because of the suffering and the loneliness that were hers in that place her name became "Hoa-make-i-ke-kula," "Companion-in-Suffering-in-the-Glade." After leading the life of a wanderer for many days she took shelter in a tree; she wrapped the vines of the tree around her, and she made up her mind that she would stay there until death came to her.

There was a man who was a king's steward, and he went to where the trees grew to get timber for the building of a house. As he went he saw something bright in an olapa tree. He went to it and looked up, and behold! there was a beautiful woman in the tree, and she was wrapped around with the ie-ie vines. The man said, "Come down, that I may speak to you; come down, wanderer." She came down from the tree. But when she stood before him he did not treat her as he would have treated a wanderer. He saw Hoa-make-i-ke-kula standing before him, and he fell at her feet, and he said: "I am indeed blest in beholding your eyes and your face and in knowing your goodness and your beauty. I beg, my Princess, that you will let me tend you."

Seeing that the man was true and good, Hoa-make-i-ke-kula let him tend her. He brought her food, and she ate, staying near the olapa tree. The man went back to his lord running and with his eyes shining. "I have seen your beautiful one in the flesh," he cried; "I have seen Hoa-make-i-ke-kula." He cried out this because he knew of the dream that his lord had had.

Then, without speaking, his lord—King Pu'u-o-nale he was—went hurrying with him to where the maiden was. She saw him, and she knew that the man of her dream was before her. Tears filled her eyes and she wept.

The King said to her, "Why do you weep, my Queen?" And she said, "I have seen one like you in my dream, time after time, and I am paying the debt of my love with my tears." And she cried, "O my sadness, and O my tears!"

Pu'u-o-nale said, "What was he like, the one you saw in your dream?" "He was like you, and his voice sounded like yours. But he was different, too; he had on his shoulder a feather cape, he had on his head a helmet of bright feathers, and he had in his hands a war club." When she said this, Pu'u-o-nale took her by the hand and brought her to his house; he put the helmet of feathers on his head, and the feather cape upon his shoulders, and he took his war club in his hand; he stood before her in this guise of a warrior, and Hoa-make-i-ke-kula knew him for the man she had seen in her dreams.

And he knew her who had appeared to him in dreams, and he took her and made her his wife. At their marriage the thunder sounded, the lightning flashed, and eight rainbows arched themselves in the heavens. These were signs from the gods that two whom they would have come together had come together at last. They lived together in Kohala, Pu'u-o-nale and Hoa-make-i-ke-kula—in Kohala, that proud land with its lonesome and loving meadows—in Kohala that is loved by its people. And in Kohala I got this story, and I have told it as it was told me there.

THE ARROW AND
THE SWING

HI-KU lived on a peak of the mountain, and Ka-we-lu lived in the lowlands. Ka-we-lu was a Princess, but at the time when she was in the lowlands she had no state nor greatness; she was alone except for some women who attended her. Hi-ku was a boy; he had a wonderful arrow that was named Pua-ne.

One day Hi-ku took his arrow and he went down toward the lowlands. He met some boys who were casting their arrows, and he offered to cast his against theirs. He cast his arrow; it went over the heads of a bald-headed man and a sightless man; it went over the heads of a lame man and a large-headed man; it went across the fields of many men, and it fell at last before the door of the girl Ka-we-lu.

Her women attendants brought the arrow to her. Ka-we-lu took it and hid it. Then Hi-ku came along. "Have any of you seen my arrow?" he said to the women attendants. "We have not seen it," they said. "The arrow fell here," said Hi-ku, "for I watched it fall." "Would you know your arrow from another arrow?" asked the Princess from her house. "Know it! Why, my arrow would answer if I called it," answered Hi-ku. "Call it, then," said the Princess. "Pua-ne, Pua-ne," Hi-ku called. "Here," said Pua-ne the arrow. "I knew you had hidden my arrow," said Hi-ku. "Come and find it," said the Princess.

He went into her house to search for the arrow, and the Princess closed the door behind him. He found the arrow. He held the arrow in his hand, and he did not go, for when he looked around he saw so many beautiful things that he forgot what he had come for.

He saw beautiful wreaths of flowers and beautiful capes of feathers; he saw mats of many beautiful colors, and he saw shells and beautiful pieces of coral. And he saw one thing that was more beautiful than all these. He saw Ka-we-lu the Princess. In the middle of her dwelling she stood, and her beauty was so bright that it seemed as if many ku-kui were blazing up with all their light. Hi-ku forgot his home on the mountain peak. He looked on the Princess, and he loved her. She had loved him when she saw him coming toward her house; but she loved him more when she saw him standing within it, his magic arrow in his hand.

He stayed in her house for five days. Every day Ka-we-lu would go into one of the houses outside and eat with her attendants. But neither on the first day nor the second day, neither on the third day nor the fourth day, nor yet on the fifth day, did she offer food to Hi-ku, nor did she tell him where he might go to get it.

He was hungry on the second day, and he became hungrier and hungrier and hungrier. He was angry on the third day, and he became angrier and angrier. And why did the Princess not offer him any food? I do not know. Some say that it was because her attendants made little of him, saying that the food they had was all for people of high rank, and that it might not be given to Hi-ku, whose rank, they said, was a low one. Perhaps her attendants prevented her giving food to him, saying such things about him.

On the fifth day, when Ka-we-lu was eating with her attendants in a house outside, Hi-ku took up his arrow and went angrily out of the house. He went toward the mountain. Then Ka-we-lu, coming out of the house where her attendants were, saw him going. She ran up the side of the mountain after him. But he went angrily on, and he never looked backward toward the Princess or toward the lowlands that she lived in.

She went swiftly after him, calling to him as the plover calls, flying here and there. She called to him, for she deeply loved him, and she looked upon him as her husband. But he, knowing that she was gaining on him, made an incantation to hold her back. He called upon the mai-le vines and the i-e vines; he called upon the ohia trees and the other branching trees to close up the path against her. But still Ka-we-lu went on, struggling against the tangle that grew across her path. Her garments were torn, and her body became covered with tears and scratches. Still she went on. But now Hi-ku was going farther and farther from her. Then she sang to him aloud, so that he could not but hear:

> "My flowers are fallen from me,
> And Hi-ku goes on and on:
> The flowers that we twined for my wreath.
> If Hi-ku would fling back to me
> A flower, since all mine are gone!"

He did not throw back a flower, nor did he call out a word to her as she followed him up the mountain ways. The vines and the branches held her, and she was not able to get through them. Then she raised her voice, and she sang to him again:

> "Do you hear, my companion, my friend!
> Ka-we-lu will live there below:
> My flowers are lost to me now:
> Down, down, far down, I will go."

Hi-ku heard what she sang. But he did not look back or make any answer. He kept on his way up the mountainside. Ka-we-lu was left behind, entangled in the vines and the branches. Afterward he was lost to her sight, and her voice could not reach him.

He went up to the peak of the mountain, and he entered his parents' house. And still he was angry. But after a night his anger went from him. And then he thought of the young Princess of Kona, with her deep eyes and her youth that was like the gush of a spring. More and more her image came before him, and he looked upon it with love.

Now one day, when he was again making his way up the mountainside, a song about himself and Ka-we-lu came into his mind. It was a song that was for Lo-lu-pe, the god who brings together friends who have been lost to each other.

> "Hi-ku is climbing the mountain ridge,
> Climbing the mountain ridge.
> The branch hangs straggling down;
> Its blossoms, flung off by Lo-lu-pe, lie on the ground.
> Give me, too, a flower, O Lo-lu-pe,
> That I may restore my wreath!"

And singing this song he went up to his parents' house.

Strangers were in the house. "Who are they, and what have they come for?" Hi-ku asked. "Ka-we-lu, the young Princess of Kona, is dead," his parents told him, "and these people have come for timbers to build a house around her dead body."

When Hi-ku heard this, he wept for his great loss. And then he left his parents and went seeking the god Lo-lu-pe, for whom he had made a song on his way up the mountain.

Now Lo-lu-pe was in the form of a kite, because he went through the air searching for things that people needed and prayed to him to find for them. And outside a wizard's house Hi-ku saw the image of Lo-lu-pe, a kite that was like a fish, and with tail and wings. Hi-ku went and said his prayer to Lo-lu-pe, and then he let the kite go in the winds.

That night Lo-lu-pe came to him in his dream, and showed him where Ka-we-lu was; she had gone down into the world that Mi-lu rules over—the world of the dead that is below the ocean. And Lo-lu-pe, in his dream, told him how he might come to her, and how he might bring Ka-we-lu's spirit back to the world of the living.

He was to take the morning-glory vines, and he was to make out of them the longest ropes that had ever been made. And to each of the long ropes he was to fix the crosspiece of a swing. Then he was to let two swings go down into the ocean's depths, and he was to lower himself by one of them. And what he was to do after that was twice told to him by Lo-lu-pe.

Hi-ku went where the morning-glory vines grew; he got the longest of the vines and, with the friends who went with him, made the longest of ropes. Then, with his friends, he went out over the ocean; he lowered the two longest ropes that were ever made, each with the crosspiece of a swing fixed to it. Down by one of the ropes Hi-ku went. And so he came to the place of the spirits, to the place at the bottom of the sea that Mi-lu rules over.

And when he came down to that place he began to swing himself on one of the swings. The spirits all saw him, and they all wanted to swing. But Hi-ku kept the swing to himself; he swung himself, and as he swung, he sang:

"I have a swing, a swing,
    And the rest of you children have none:
    Whom will I let on my swing?
    Not one of this crowd, not one."

The spirit of Ka-we-lu was standing there beside Mi-lu, the King. Hi-ku saw her amongst the crowd of spirits. But Ka-we-lu did not know Hi-ku.

Mi-lu came to where Hi-ku was swinging. He wanted to go on the swing. Hi-ku gave him the seat. Then the spirits began to swing him, and Mi-lu was so delighted with the swinging that he had all the spirits pull on the ropes to swing him—the ropes that were on the crosspiece and that were for pulling.

Then Hi-ku went to Ka-we-lu. "Here is our swing," he said, and he brought her where the second vine rope was hanging. He put her on the seat, and he began to swing her. And as he swung her he chanted as they chant in the upper world, the world of the living, when one is being swung:

"Wounded is Wai-mea by the piercing wind;
The bud of the purple ohai is drooping;
Jealous and grieved is the flower of the ko-aie;
Pained is the wood of Wai-ka;
O Love! Wai-ka loves me as a lover;
Like unto a lover is the flower of Koo-lau;
It is the flower in the woods of Ma-he-le.
The wood is a place for journeying,
The wild pili grass has its place in the forests,
Life is but a simple round at Ka-hua.
O Love! Love it was which came to me;
Whither has it vanished?
O Love! Farewell."

He chanted this, thinking that Ka-we-lu would remember her days in the upper world when she heard what was chanted at the swinging games. But Ka-we-lu did not remember.

Then Hi-ku went on the swing. "Come and swing with me," he said, when he got on the seat. "Sit upon my knees," he said, "and I will cover myself with my mantle."

Ka-we-lu jumped up, and she sat upon Hi-ku's knees. They began to swing backward and forward, backward and forward, while Mi-lu, the King of the Dead, was being swung by the spirits. Then Hi-ku pulled on the morning-glory vine. This was a signal; his friends did as he had told them to do; they began to pull up the swing. Up, up, came Hi-ku, and up came Ka-we-lu, held in Hi-ku's arms.

But Ka-we-lu shrank and shrank as she came up near the sunlight; she shrank until she was smaller than a girl, smaller than a child; until she was smaller than a bird, even. Hi-ku and she came to the surface of the ocean. Then he, holding her, went back in his canoe and came to where, the timbers built around it, her body was laid. He brought the spirit to the body, the spirit that had shrunken, and he held the spirit to the soles of the body's feet. The spirit went in at the soles of the feet; it passed up; it came to the breast; it came to the throat. Having reached the throat, the spirit stayed in the body. Then the body was taken up by Hi-ku; it was warmed, and afterward Ka-we-lu was as she had been before. Then these two, Ka-we-lu and Hi-ku, lived long together in a place between the mountain and the lowlands, and they wove many wreaths for each other, and they sang many songs to each other, and they left offerings for Lo-lu-pe often—for Lo-lu-pe, who brings to the people knowledge of where their lost things are.

THE ROLLING
ISLAND

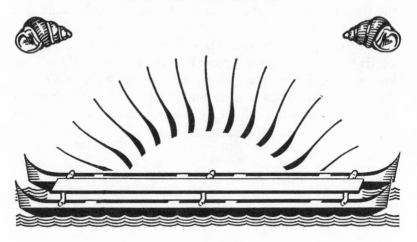

I.

THERE are islands that appear and disappear, not because they rise up from the depths of the ocean and sink down again, but because they are rolled here and there by one or another of the gods. They are sacred islands and it is unlucky to point to them, unlucky to look long at them when they appear. One is tinged with red: it can be seen only in the sunrise or the sunset. The Hawaiians before they turn their heads away say its name: it is Ulu-ka-a, the Rolling Island.

Would you hear about that island? There is a story that begins with one who was a Chief on our island a long time ago. His name was Ka-ewe-aoho. His two fishermen were the ones among his attendants whom he favored most, for fishing was this Chief's favorite pursuit. He would be pleased when his fishermen would let him go in their canoe to the far-off fishing grounds. But this they would do only when the sea was very smooth.

They were rough men who seldom spoke to Ka-ewe-aoho about anything, and who thought only of lines and paddles, of their canoe and the fish they were out to get; when they were on the land they wanted only to eat and sleep. But the Chief's steward grew jealous of them. When they were a whole day out at sea with him, what did they tell him, he asked himself, and did they get him to do this and that which the steward did not want him to do? His jealousy grew and grew. He thought of a way of making them go away from Ka-ewe-aoho's lands so that they would no longer be his fishermen.

Once when, without Ka-ewe-aoho, they had been a long day out at sea, the fishermen came to their house and found no food had been left for them. They were angry, thinking that their Chief had neglected them. It was now the season when the sea was not smooth and they did not see him. And night after night when they had come back with a catch of fish they found no food in their house. It was because the steward had given to others the food Ka-ewe-aoho had portioned out for his fishermen.

They took some of the catch that belonged to their Chief to feed themselves. And they got more and more angry. So angry did they grow that one night as they sat foodless in their house they planned to destroy Ka-ewe-aoho.

The next day he came to ask them to let him go with them to the far-off fishing grounds. They said, "Yes; today the sea is smooth and you can go with us." They made ready to deal treacherously with him. There were the two paddles and the two bailers in the canoe, but under the fishing tackle they had hidden two other paddles.

They paddled out until the land was out of sight, Ka-ewe-aoho with them. "See the white caps yonder! The best fishing is there," they told him when he asked them to begin fishing. And when they got to that point the fishermen began to carry out their revengeful plan. One dropped his paddle saying that a wave had swept it out of his hand. Then the other paddle was dropped into the sea. Ka-ewe-aoho saw them being carried away by the waves. He said, "I am the youngest man here. Let me swim after the paddles. When I bring them back we can go safely home." He swam after the paddles. Then the fishermen took the ones they had hidden and began to paddle toward the land.

Ka-ewe-aoho cried out to them, "Stay and save your Chief," and as they went farther from him, he cried, "If I have wronged you I shall right the wrong. I shall give you lands. Save me or I drown!" But the canoe sped farther and farther from him. He wept for his fate. He ceased to swim and let himself float on the water. The canoe of the faithless fishermen was now out of sight and he thought there was no hope for him. But as he floated a rainbow bent above him and a reddish glow shone around him. And this was because he was a Chief of high rank, a descendant of the Heavenly Ones.

II.

Ku, in the Country that Supports the Heavens, looking down on the ocean, saw the rainbow and the reddish glow and knew that a mortal who was a descendant of the Heavenly Ones was abandoned there. "This one," he said, "would be a fitting husband for my grandchild A-ne-li-ke who is on Ulu-ka-a with women attendants who have never seen a man. I will roll the island toward this Chief. He will go on it and be saved; my favorite grandchild will find him there."

Then Ka-ewe-aoho, already spent, heard waves breaking on a land. Just as his strength was failing utterly a breaker rolled him upon the soft sand. There he lay as one dead. And when life came back to him he was astonished to find himself upon land. But what land? He could see no houses, no people, no cultivated patches, no canoes on the beach. Night was coming on now and he went into a hole under a tree where he slept.

When it was daylight he went across the land and saw that it was an island shaped like a breadfruit. And although there were no cultivated patches to be seen there was food growing on the island. He saw a banana tree with bunches of ripened fruit. He went to it, plucked and began to eat the fruit.

It was then that A-ne-li-ke, Ku's grandchild, came upon him. She thought that this stranger was beautiful. Then when she saw him eating she ran toward him saying, "Do not eat that for it is fit only for rats. It is poison for such as you!" Ka-ewe-aoho was astonished to see such a beautiful creature before him. "I fear to speak to you," he said, "for my words will seem to you like the squeaking of rats." "Your words are like the songs of birds," she said. "I understand all you say. Where have you come from?" He showed her the sea, and she said softly, "Man-from-the-Sea!" So hungry he was that he went on eating from the bunch in his hands. "Man-from-the-Sea, do not eat that," she said. He asked her, "What do you eat?" "Berries," she said. "My attendants have gone to the mountain to gather berries. But I have gourds and gourds filled with berries in my house. Come there, Man-from-the-Sea, and eat food that is fit for you."

He went with her, looking at her wonderingly; never had he seen on broad Hawaii a woman as beautiful as she was. As they went along he saw yams and breadfruit and sugercane growing wild. He gathered them. But she, he could see, was ashamed that he should do this. Still, his hunger was so great that he could not help but gather this food, hoping that he would be able to cook it. He saw sticks that made fire when they were rubbed together. He took up these, too. "Man-from-the-Sea, will you eat them?" she asked. "No," he told her. "These make fire." "Fire!" she said, and he knew that she had never heard the word, never had seen the blaze of fire.

They came to her house and she went within to get food that was fit for Man-from-the-Sea—berries. While she was within he built an oven and put the breadfruit and the yams in it. Then he began to work with the sticks so as to make fire, rubbing them together very hard.

It was strange work that Man-from-the-Sea was doing, she thought. Then a spark came from the rubbing. It went among the leaves that he had made ready for it. There was smoke, there was smoldering, and then there was a blaze. A-ne-li-ke was affrighted. She threw more wood on it thinking to drive the fire away. And then it blazed up in Ka-ewe-aoho's face, burning his eyebrows.

But he put the food in, heated the oven and covered it over. After a while he took the food out; when he began to eat it she watched him in terror, thinking that he would be both burned and poisoned by it. Yet she saw that as he ate it he seemed more and more pleased. He offered her some and she tasted it. Then she took more of it. "Man-from-the-Sea, what you have brought us is good," she said.

They did not see her attendants approach. They were coming to the house with loads of berries, and when they saw a stranger with A-ne-li-ke they hid themselves behind trees so as to be ready to save her when he would try to harm her. But even as these women attendants watched him they said to each other "How beautiful he is!" Then they saw him give her steaming food and saw her eat it. They began to wail. "O one whom we have guarded, do not die, do not take poison," they wailed. A-ne-li-ke told them that what she ate was good. They ceased wailing, and when they tasted the cooked food themselves they liked it. No longer were they afraid of Man-from-the-Sea. "How beautiful he is!" they said. "And if he has done good to you, A-ne-li-ke, you should take him for your husband." And after some time they told her, "You must go to your grandfather in the Country that Supports the Heavens and ask his permission to marry your Man-from-the-Sea."

III.

Then A-ne-li-ke's attendants planted in the ground the sacred coconut; over it they chanted:

> "O life-giving coconut
> That budded in Kahiki,
> That rooted in Kahiki,
> That formed a trunk in Kahiki,
> That bore leaves in Kahiki,
> That bore fruit in Kahiki,
> That ripened in Kahiki."

All at once the shoot of a tree sprouted from the ground. It became a high tree. A-ne-li-ke seated herself amongst the leaves and held on tightly. Higher and higher grew the tree until to Man-from-the-Sea the leaves looked like dots in the sky. She called down "My hands and my feet are stiff with fear!" Her attendants called out, "O life-giving coconut, hold fast the grandchild of Ku!" Then A-ne-li-ke lost her fear for a while for the power that was Ku's came into her. But as the tree went higher and higher she called down again, "My hands and my feet are stiff with fear!" Faintly her voice came to them, "My hands and my feet . . ." and her attendants called out, "O life-giving coconut, hold fast the grandchild of Ku!" Higher and higher went the tree, and at last it bent over on the Country that Supports the Heavens. Downward then it bent until the leaves touched the ground. Then A-ne-li-ke went upon the land. The tree grew smaller and went out of her sight.

She went upon a paved way until she came to a royal house; there, as she knew, her grandfather, Ku, dwelt. She went within, and he, when he saw a stranger in his sacred house went to seize her, anger in his heart. But when he laid his hands on her he felt the power that was in her and he fell backward. "Why did you

come without my being told?" he asked. "You are my grandchild. Come now and sit upon my lap."

So A-ne-li-ke went and sat on his sacred lap. She told him that
she had come to gain his permission to marry Man-from-the-
Sea. Then Ku said, "Not you but I drew that man to the island.
The signs of a divinely-descended Chief were about him as he
struggled in the water, and I knew that he would be a fit husband
for you, my grandchild. Therefore go back to Ulu-ka-a and take
Man-from-the-Sea for your husband. But know that it is not
well for the mortals who marry with the Divine Ones."

Holding her hands he let his own arms stretch out, stretch
down until A-ne-li-ke was once more upon the ground. She was
on Ulu-ka-a once more. She told her attendants that it was Ku's
will that she should marry Man-from-the-Sea. "All then is
well," they said. "We have come to like Man-from-the-Sea. If
your grandfather would not have you, his favorite grandchild,
marry this mortal, we would have had your younger sister, Ka-
ahi-wela, marry him—she who is on another island." But A-ne-
li-ke was not pleased to hear them speak of Man-from-the-Sea's
marrying this younger sister.

So they wed, the Chief of Hawaii and the grandchild of Ku.
Very happy they were, weaving wreaths for each other, wandering through Ulu-ka-a, the Rolling Island. And Ka-ewe-aoho no
longer remembered his life on broad Hawaii. But his sisters
remembered him. They thought and thought about him and
they thought so longingly about him that their thoughts reached
to his mind. Once as he wandered away from A-ne-li-ke's house
he came to the place where the breaker had thrown him. There
he lay on the warm sand and a deep sleep came over him. And in
that sleep he saw his sisters and he heard their voices. "You
are living in peace with your beautiful wife, and far away are
your people who go up and down the land mourning for you."
And his sisters' voices said, "Your temple has been desecrated;
your sacred landing place is overrun with common people; your

parents mourn for you so that they are not able to eat, and sleep does not visit them. O Chief of Hawaii, beloved by all, sleep now, but when you awaken think upon the land that once you had such love for."

Three times he saw his sisters in a dream and three times they said the same words to him. Each time when he awakened he was surprised that it was a dream, so clearly he had seen them and so clearly he had heard his sisters' voices. Now he was no longer content to wander through Ulu-ka-a with A-ne-li-ke and weave wreaths for her. Often he was sad and tears would come into his eyes.

Once his wife said to him, "Are you not content with me? Or is it that you think my youngest sister is more beautiful than I am and that you would be happy weaving wreaths for her?" But he said, "I do not think upon your sister whom I have never seen. I think upon the land I came from. There I was Chief in Hawaii, and the people mourn me there." And he said again, "I live here in peace with you, my beautiful wife, but I cannot be happy until I see my land and my people again."

She said to him, "Wait until old age dims your eyes before you leave my island for your own land."

Another time when he had wandered away from her and she found him lying on the warm sand, he said to her, "My love for you is great, but I cannot stay away from my people. Show me how I can get to them. If I leave you and if a son is born to us name him Eyebrows-burnt-off because my eyebrows were burnt off when you tried to quench my first fire."

Knowing that he was not satisfied to stay with her, A-ne-li-ke ordered that a canoe be built for him. In one day it was all ready: at sunrise her attendants cut down the tree and at sunset the canoe with its sails and paddles was on the water. The next day A-ne-li-ke and Ka-ewe-aoho went down to it and took farewell of each other there. The canoe was red, with red mast and red ropes and red sails, and those who manned it were all in red.

And when he went into the canoe she warned him not to look
back: he was to take no glimpse of Ulu-ka-a once his canoe
started for Hawaii. He stood with his back to the Rolling
Island until, at sunset, the canoe came to Hawaii. When he
stepped upon the landing place the attendants sped the canoe
away from Hawaii. Ka-ewe-aoho's people saw him and hailed
him. They bore him to his royal house. His parents were there;
they were wasted with mourning for him. But they grew well
and rejoiced when the Chief's sacred landing place became his
again and when the temple that had been desecrated was
restored.

IV.

So the Chief lived on broad Hawaii. And on Ulu-ka-a, the
Rolling Island, his wife bore a son. She named him Eyebrows-
burnt-off. Very rapidly he grew up, and soon the women attendants of his mother were not able to control him. Then one
day he said to his mother, "Where is my father?"

"You have no father," A-ne-li-ke told him.

"I must have a father," he said, "I am named Eyebrows-
burnt-off because of what happened to my father." And again
he asked, "Where is he?"

A-ne-li-ke knew that her son would have to be told where his
father was, and being told he would want to go there. "He is
a Chief in Hawaii," she said. "I have to seek him," Eyebrows-
burnt-off said. "If I die while doing so, it is well; if I live to find
him, it is well also. But I must go where he is."

So A-ne-li-ke had a canoe built for her son. Once again a tree
was cut down at sunrise and once again a canoe was in the water
at sunset. Eyebrows-burnt-off went into it. The canoe was red;
the mast and ropes and sails were red, and the attendants were
all in red. And as Eyebrows-burnt-off went into the canoe taking farewell of her, his mother warned him that he must not look

back on Ulu-ka-a. They sailed away at sunrise and at sunset
they came to Hawaii. Eyebrows-burnt-off had not looked back.

As the canoe came near the people who were on the beach said,
"No man, woman or child must be permitted to desecrate our
Chief's landing place. If one in the red canoe goes upon it we
must kill him."

Eyebrows-burnt-off went upon the strand and the canoe sped
away from Hawaii. Then he went upon the Chief's landing
place. People rushed to seize him. The boy leaped across their
heads. They tore his dress. But he outdistanced them and went
to the Chief's enclosure. The guards struck him as he went into
the house.

The Chief was seated on his mats, his attendants were fan-
ning him when this stranger boy threw himself amongst them.
Before they knew what he was there for he seated himself on the
Chief's lap. "Who is this stranger? Why has he been let come
upon my lap? Death is due to the stranger who has done this."

Then said the boy on the Chief's lap. "I am Eyebrows-burnt-
off, and my mother, A-ne-li-ke sends her greetings to you, my
father." Ka-ewe-aoho recognized his son. He wept over him and
questioned him about the wife he had left on Ulu-ka-a, the Rolling Island. And all that night he thought of his beautiful wife
whom he could find no way of going back to. In days afterward
he showed his son what one should do who would be Chief in
Hawaii.

V.

So it was on broad Hawaii, and on Ulu-ka-a, the Rolling
Island, A-ne-li-ke thought about Man-from-the-Sea and wondered if his love for her still lasted. She would find out, and if
it did she would bring him back to live with her on Ulu-ka-a
until age dimmed his eyes. She rolled the island to where the
other grandchildren of Ku, her eleven sisters, lived, each on her

own island. She brought them all on Ulu-ka-a. There they lived, eating cooked food and pondering on what was told them about Man-from-the-Sea who had come there, who had been a husband to their sister, who had been the father of a son she had borne. And the eleven sisters said to each other, "Why did not our grandfather Ku cause a Man-from-the-Sea to come on the islands that we lived on?" Then one day A-ne-li-ke ordered her attendants to build a great canoe. A great tree was cut down at sunrise and at sunset a great canoe was in the water; it was red and its mast and ropes and sails were red. At sunrise they went into the canoe, A-ne-li-ke and her eleven sisters, all in red they were, and they sailed across the sea to Hawaii.

"What a beautiful woman!" the people cried out as each of them went upon the Chief's landing place. And word was brought to Ka-ewe-aoho about the red canoe and the women who had come in it.

Said Eyebrows-burnt-off to his father. "My mother means to try if your love for her has lasted. If she finds it has not she will strike you dead. Each of Ku's grandchildren will come to you, and if you are not able to distinguish A-ne-li-ke amongst them you will live no longer than today. This is what you must do: have eleven houses ready and have each of her sisters sent to one of them; have A-ne-li-ke herself stay with you. To each of the others say, 'You are not as beautiful as A-ne-li-ke's neck, or her ankle, or her knee, or her eyes, or some other part of her.' And if you are able to know A-ne-li-ke from the others you will live to go with her back to Ulu-ka-a, the Rolling Island."

One after another beautiful women came before the Chief, each claiming to be his wife. Each would sit on his lap. But the Chief said to this one and that one, "You are not as beautiful as A-ne-li-ke's eyes, or her hair, or her ankle, or her knee," and each went away ashamed. One was so like A-ne-li-ke as he first knew her that he nearly took her upon his lap. Then he remembered how his wife used to fix her eyes on him, and this woman's eyes were cast down. "All your body has not the beauty of A-ne-li-ke's arm," he said, and she went away ashamed. This was Ka-ahi-wela, the youngest of Ku's grandchildren.

A woman came before him and when he looked on her he knew that she was A-ne-li-ke. He wept and she went and sat upon his lap. "Your life is spared," she said.

In his house they lived for a while. Then a day came when A-ne-li-ke told her husband that they should go to her own island. Ka-ewe-aoho then gave the chiefship to his son, and going in the great canoe sailed away with Ku's grandchildren, eleven of whom kept their faces hidden from him. They came to Ulu-ka-a, the Rolling Island; then each of the eleven went to her own island. And as for A-ne-li-ke, she and her Man-from-the-Sea lived in peace for many years. When Ka-ewe-aoho came back to Hawaii his son was an old man.

THE DAUGHTER
OF THE KING OF
KU-AI-HE-LANI

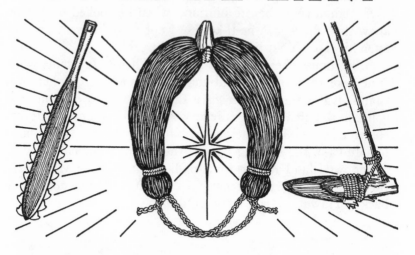

THE Country that Supports the Heavens, Ku-ai-he-lani,
was where Maki-i lived and ruled as King. He came to
one of our islands, and there he took a wife. After a while
he had to go back to Ku-ai-he-lani, and before he went he said
this to the woman he had married: "I know that a daughter will
be born to us. I would have you name the girl Lau-kia-manu.
If, when you have brought her up, she has a desire to come to
live with me, let her make the journey to Ku-ai-he-lani. But she
must come in a red canoe with red sails and red cords, with red
bailing cups, and with men in red to have charge of it. And she
must be accompanied by a large canoe and a small canoe, by
big men and by little men. And give her these; they will be
tokens by which I shall know her for my daughter—this necklace of whales' teeth, this bracelet, and this bright feather

cloak." Maki-i then gave the tokens to his wife, and he departed for the land of Ku-ai-he-lani.

A child was born to the wife whom he had left behind, and she named the child Lau-kia-manu. Meanwhile Maki-i in his own land had planted a garden and had filled it with lovely flowers, and another garden and had filled it with pleasant fruits, and had made a bathing pool; he made the gardens and the pool forbidden places to everyone except the daughter who might come to him in Ku-ai-he-lani. And he had instructed the guards about the tokens by which they would know Lau-kia-manu, his daughter.

The girl grew up under her mother's care. As she grew older she began to ask about her father—who was he and where had he gone to? And once when she asked about him, her mother said to her: "Go to the cliff yonder; that is your father." The child went to the cliff and asked: "Are you my father?" The cliff denied it and said, "I am not your father." The child came back and craved of her mother, again, to tell her who her father was. "Go to the bamboo bush yonder," said her mother; "that is your father." The child went to the bamboo bush and said, "Are you my father?" "I am not," said the bamboo bush. "Maki-i is your father." "And where is he?" said the child. "He has gone back to Ku-ai-he-lani."

She went back and said to her mother, "Maki-i is my father, and he is in the land of Ku-ai-he-lani, and you have hidden this from me." Her mother said: "I have hidden it because if you went to visit him terrible things would befall you. For he told me that you should go to him in a red canoe with red sails and red cords, with red bailing cups, and with men in red to have charge of it. And he said that you should be accompanied by a large canoe and a small canoe, by big men and little men. He gave me tokens for you to bring also, but there is no use in giving you these, for you cannot go except in the canoes he spoke of, and there is no way by which you can come by possessions that denote such royal state."

So her mother said, but Lau-kia-manu still had thoughts of going to Ku-ai-he-lani, where her father was King. She grew to be a girl, and then one day she said to her mother, "I have no way by which I can come into possession of canoes that would denote my royal state, but for all that I will make a journey to Ku-ai-he-lani; I will not remain here." Her mother said, "Go if you will, but terrible things will befall you." And then her mother said: "Go on and on until you come to where two old women are roasting bananas by the wayside. They are your grandmother and your grandaunt. Reach down and take away the bananas they are roasting. Let them search for them until they ask who has taken them. Tell them then who you are. When they ask 'What brings you this way?' say, 'I have come because I must have a roadway.' When you say this to them, your grandmother and your grandaunt will give you a roadway to Ku-ai-he-lani."

Lau-kia-manu left her mother and went upon her way. She came where the two old women were by the wayside, and she did as her mother had told her. "Whose offspring are you?" asked the old women. "Your own," said Lau-kia-manu, and she told them the name of her mother. "What brings you, lady, to us here?" asked the old women. And the girl answered, "I have come to you because I want a roadway."

Thereupon one of the old women said: "Here is a roadway; it is this bamboo stalk. Climb to the top of it, and when it leans over it will reach into Ku-ai-he-lani." Lau-kia-manu went to the top of the bamboo stalk and sat there. It began to shoot up. When it reached a great height it leaned over; the end of it reached Ku-ai-he-lani, the Country that Supports the Heavens.

Lau-kia-manu then went along until she came to a garden that was filled with lovely flowers. She went into it. There grew the ilima and the me-le ku-le and the mai-le vine. She gathered the vines and the flowers, and she twined them into wreaths for herself. And she went from that garden into another garden. There all kinds of pleasant fruits were growing. She plucked and she ate of them. She saw beyond that garden the clear, cool surface of a pool. She went there; she undressed herself, and she bathed in that pool. And when she was in the water there, a turtle came and rubbed her back.

She dressed, and she sat on the edge of the pool. And then the guards who had been placed over the flower garden and the fruit garden and the bathing pool came to where she was. "You are indeed a strange girl," they said to her, "for you have plucked the flowers and the fruit in the gardens that are forbidden to all except the King's daughter, and you have bathed in the pool that is for her alone. You will certainly die for doing these things."

The guards went to Maki-i: they told him about the strange girl and what she had done. The King ordered that they should tie her hands and stand guard over her all night, and that when the dawn came they should take her to the seashore and slay her there.

The guards took Lau-kia-manu; they tied her hands, they flung her into a pigpen, and they remained on watch over her all night. At midnight an owl came and perched over where the girl lay. Then the owl called out to her:

> "Say, Lau-kia-manu,
> Daughter of Maki-i!
> Do you know what will befall you?
> Die you will, die you must!"

To that the girl made answer:

> "Wicked owl, wicked owl!
> You are bad indeed,
> Thus to reveal me:

Lau-kia-manu, Lau-kia-manu,
Daughter of Maki-i."

The call of the owl and the answer of the girl came twice before
the guards heard them. Then they stood up and they listened.
They heard the call again, and they heard the answer of the girl
within the pigpen. Then one of the guards said, "This must be
Lau-kia-manu, the King's own daughter; we must tell him about
it all." But the other guard said: "No. Lau-kia-manu, the
King's daughter, was to come in a red canoe, having red sails,
red cords, and red bailing cups, with men in red in charge, and
with a large canoe, a small canoe, big men, and little men ac-
companying it. This is a low-class girl; she has come with none
of these things." The owl spoke again, and the girl made answer,
and when they heard what was said the guards agreed that they
should go to the King and tell him all that they had heard.

The King went back with the two guards. The owl was still
above the pigpen, and the girl still within it. The owl called out:

"Say, Lau-kia-manu,
Daughter of Maki-i!
Do you know what will befall you?
Die you will, die you must!"

And to that the girl made answer:

"Wicked owl, wicked owl!
You are bad indeed,
Thus to reveal me:
Lau-kia-manu, Lau-kia-manu,
Daughter of Maki-i."

When the King heard this he went into the pigpen.

Now, after the guards had gone to inform the King of what
they had heard the owl flew down upon Lau-kia-manu; it

clapped its wings over the girl; it placed the necklace of whales' teeth around her neck, it placed the bracelet upon her arm, it put the cloak of bright feathers around her. For this owl was really her grandaunt, and it was to her that Lau-kia-manu's mother had given the tokens by which the girl was to be recognized when she came into Maki-i's kingdom.

When her father broke into the pigpen he saw her standing there with the necklace of whales' teeth around her neck, with the bracelet upon her wrist, and with the cloak of bright feathers around her. He took her up and he wept over her; he gave her the garden of flowers and the garden of fruits and the bathing pool with the clear cool water. Then, in a while, he brought Ula to her.

Ula was a prince from Kahiki-ku, and he was as handsome as she was lovely. What a sight it was to see them together, Lau-kia-manu and Ula, the Prince from Kahiki-ku! "What light is that in yonder house?" he had said to her father on the night that he came to Ku-ai-he-lani. "That is not a light," said Maki-i; "it is the radiance of the woman who is within." He brought Ula into the house, and Ula and Lau-kia-manu met.

For fifty days they were together. Then Ula had to return to his own land, to Kahiki-ku. "You cannot go there unless you take me with you," said Lau-kia-manu. "You cannot come with me," said Ula. "If you came you would meet with terrible suffering at the hands of the Queen of Kahiki-ku."

He went back to his own land. Lau-kia-manu remained in Ku-ai-he-lani, but she was so overcome by her love for Ula that, every morning when she saw the clouds in the sky drifting toward Kahiki-ku, she would chant this poem:

> "The sun is up, it is up:
> My love is ever up before me:
> Love is a burthen when one is in love,
> And falling tears are its due."

She would weep then. And when she found out that she could not put her love away from her, either by night or by day, she went down to the seashore and she wept there. Then, when her weeping was at an end, she called out, "O turtle with the shiny back, O my grandmother of the sea, come to me."

The turtle with the shiny back appeared. She opened her shell at her back. Lau-kia-manu went within the shell. Then the turtle went under the water. She swam under the sea, and she swam on and on until she came with Lau-kia-manu to the land of Kahiki-ku. The girl stepped on the seashore, and the turtle dived into the ocean and disappeared.

Lau-kia-manu went along by the seashore. She came to where there was a fish pond that belonged to the Queen of Kahiki-ku. She stayed beside the fish pond while she uttered a charm, saying:

"Ye forty thousand gods,
  Ye four hundred thousand gods,
  Ye rows of gods,
  Ye assemblies of gods,
  Ye older brothers of the gods,
  Ye fourfold gods,
  Ye fivefold gods,
    Take away from me my beauty, make it hidden:
    Give me the form of a crone, bowed and blear-eyed."

And when she had said that, her beauty was taken away from her, and she appeared as an old woman, bent and wandering, with a stick in her hand, gathering sea eggs.

In the fish pond there were many kinds of silver fish. Lau-kia-manu uttered a spell, and caused them all to disappear a minute after she had seen them swimming about. Still she stayed near, dragging herself here and there about the seashore. And while she was there, messengers came to bring from the Queen's pond silver fish for the Queen.

There was not a single fish in the pond. When the messengers saw this, they accused the old woman who was nearby of having taken the fish out of the pond. She made no reply to them. Then nothing would do the messengers but to take her before the Queen and charge her with having stolen the silver fish out of her pond.

So they brought her before the Queen. "There is not a single fish in your pond," they said, "and we found this old woman near it, going up and down." The Queen said, "Nothing will happen to you, old woman, if you will take as your name the name of my sickness." The old woman said that she would do that. Then the Queen named her Li-pe-wa-le, the name of the Queen's sickness; she let her stay in the house, and she gave her food.

So Lau-kia-manu became known as Li-pe-wa-le. In the Queen's house she did menial tasks. And into the house came the Prince who was to wed the Queen. He was Ula. Once when she was lying on her mat asleep, Ula came and kissed Lau-kia-manu. She wakened up and cried out, "Who is kissing me?" The Queen heard her voice and said, "What is it, Li-pe-wa-le?" Lau-kia-manu made no answer. We can see by what Ula did that he knew his sweetheart of Ku-ai-he-lani in spite of her being transformed into an old woman.

One day the Queen went down to the seashore to bathe. She bade Li-pe-wa-le stay within the house and decorate a dress that she was to wear. Li-pe-wa-le did as she was ordered. But she worked so quickly on the dress that she had it all done very soon, and she was able to follow the Queen and her attendants down to the seashore. And on her way she caused herself to be transformed back into her own shape, with her own beauty. She passed the others by; she bathed near where the Queen bathed, and the Queen and all her attendants were able to look upon her. Then she dressed herself and hurried away.

They all hurried after her; the Queen was angry that one who was more beautiful than she was should be in her country. Lau-kia-manu went more quickly than they did, and when they came to the Queen's house she had already transformed herself, and the only one they saw there was Li-pe-wa-le, the old and withered woman.

That night the Queen and her attendants and Ula the Prince went to dance in a house that the Queen had built. She put on her beautiful wreaths with the dress that Li-pe-wa-le had decorated for her. But she ordered Li-pe-wa-le to stay within the house and decorate another dress.

There she stayed, and the sounds of the music and the dancing came to her. And then the girl went without. She looked over to the house where the dance was going on, and she uttered this charm:

> "Ye forty thousand gods,
>   Ye four hundred thousand gods,
>   Ye rows of gods,
>   Ye assemblies of gods,
>   Ye older brothers of the gods,
>   Ye gods that whisper,
>   Ye gods that watch by night,
>   Ye gods that show your gleaming eyes by night,
>   Come down, awake, make a move, stir yourselves!
>   There is the house, the house."

And when she uttered this spell the Queen, who was dancing, fell down on the ground. Fire burst out all around the house. And then Lau-kia-manu, in the light of the fires, in the light of her own beauty, stood in the doorway of the house. Ula the Prince saw her there. "Come to me, oh, come to me, beautiful woman," he said. But Lau-kia-manu made answer: "I will not go to you now, nor ever again. In your own country you did not cherish me, but you left me to sorrow and affliction. Now I go back to Ku-ai-he-lani." So she left the burning house, and she went down to the seashore. She called upon the turtle with the shiny back, her grandmother of the sea; and the turtle came and opened the shell on her back, and Lau-kia-manu went within it. And she journeyed through the ocean, under the waves, and came back again to the land of Ku-ai-he-lani, and there ever afterward she stayed.

THE WOMAN
FROM LALO-
HANA

THE COUNTRY UNDER THE SEA

L ONG, long ago, my younger brothers, there lived in Hawaii a King whose name was Koni-konia. He sent his fishermen out to catch deep-sea fish for him, and they, without knowing it, let down their lines and fishhooks at a place where, before this, strange things had happened.

In a while after they had let them down, the hooks were taken off the lines. The fishermen wondered at this, for they knew that no fish had bitten at their baits. They went back to the King, and they told him what had happened. There had come no quiver on their lines, they said, as there would have come if fish had touched their baits, and their hooks had been cut off the lines as if some one with a knife had done it.

Now the King had heard before of strange things happening

at the place in the sea where the fishermen had been; and after they had shown him the lines with the hooks cut off, he sent for a wizard, that he might learn from him how these strange things had come to be.

The wizard (he was called a Kahuna) came before the King, and after he had been told of what had happened to the fishermen's lines he said: "Your fishermen let their lines down over Lalo-hana, a country that is at the bottom of the sea, just under the place where they let their canoes rest. A woman lives there, a very beautiful woman of the sea whose name is Hina; all alone she lives there, for her brothers, who were given charge of her, have gone to a place far off." When the King heard of this beautiful woman of the sea, he longed to see her and to have her for his wife.

The Kahuna told him how she might be brought out of the sea to him. The King was to have a great many images made— images of a man, each image to be as large as a man, with pearl-shell eyes and dark hair, and with a malo or dress around it. Some of the images were to be brought out to sea, and some of them were to be left on the beach and along a path that went up to the King's house; and one of them was to be left standing by the door of the house.

The Kahuna went with the men who had taken the images in their canoes. When they came to that part of the sea that the country of Lalo-hana was under, the Kahuna told the men to let down one of the images. Down, down, the image went, a rope around it. It rested on the bottom of the sea. Then another image was let down. But this image was not let as far as the bottom of the sea: it was held about the height of a house above the bottom. Then another image was let down and held above that, and then another image, and another image, all held one above another, while other images were left standing in canoes that went in a line back to the beach. And when all the images were in their places, a loud trumpet was blown.

The Woman of Lalo-hana, Hina, came out of her house, that was built of white and red coral, and she saw the image of a man of dark color, with dark hair and eyes of pearl shell, standing before her. She was pleased, for she had never seen even the likeness of a man since her brothers had gone away from her; and she went to the image, and she touched it. As she did so she saw an image above her; and she went and she touched this image too. And all the way up to the top of the sea there were images; and Hina went upward, touching them all.

When she came up to the surface of the sea she saw canoes, and in each canoe there was an image standing. Each one seemed to be more beautiful than the others; and Hina swam on and on, gazing on each with delight and touching this one and that one.

And so Hina, the Woman of the Sea, came to the beach. And on the beach there were other images; and she went on, touching each of them. And so she went through the grove of coconut trees and came before the King's house. Outside the house there was a very tall image with very large pearl-shell eyes and with a red malo around it. Hina went to that image. The wreath of sea flowers that she had in her hair was now withered with the sun; the Woman of Lalo-hana was wearied now, and she lay down beside the image and fell asleep.

When she wakened it was not the image, but the King, who was beside her. She saw him move his hands, and she was frightened because of the movements she saw him make and the sounds that were around her after the quiet of the sea. Her wreath of sea flowers was all shriveled up in the sunlight. The man kissed her, and they went together into the house.

And so the Woman of Lalo-hana, the Country under the Sea, came to Hawaii and lived there as the wife of Koni-konia, the King.

After a while, when she had learned to speak to him, Hina told Koni-konia about precious things that she had in her house in Lalo-hana, the Country under the Sea, and she begged the

King to send a diver to get these things and bring them to her. They were in a calabash within her house, she said. And she told the King that the diver who brought it up was not to open the calabash.

So Koni-konia the King sent the best of his divers to go down to Lalo-hana, the Country under the Sea, and bring up the calabash that had Hina's precious things in it. The diver went down, and found the house of red and white coral, and went within and took the calabash that was there. He brought it back without opening it and gave it to Hina.

After some days Hina opened the calabash. Within it was the moon. It flew up to the heavens, and there it shone clear and bright. When it shone in the heavens it was called *Kena*. But it shone down on the sea too, and shining on the sea it was called *Ana*.

And then, seeing *Ana* in the sea, the Woman of Lalo-hana was frightened. "My brothers will come searching for me," she said. And the next day she said, "My brothers will bring a great flood of waters upon this land when they come searching for me." And after that she said, "My brothers will seek me in the forms of pa-o'o fishes, and the Ocean will lift them up so that they can go seeking me." When the King heard her say this he said, "We will go far from where the Ocean is, and we will seek refuge on the tops of the mountains."

So the King with Hina, with all his people, went to the mountains. As they went they saw the Ocean lifting up. Hina's brothers in the forms of pa-o'o fishes were there, and the Ocean lifted them up that they might go seeking her.

Over the land and up to the mountains the Ocean went, bearing the pa-o'o fishes along. Koni-konia and his people climbed to the tops of the mountains. To the tops of the mountains the Ocean went, bearing the pa-o'o fishes that were Hina's brothers. Koni-konia and Hina and all the people climbed to the tops of the trees that were on the tops of the mountains. And then the

Ocean, having covered the tops of the mountains, went back again, drawing back the pa-o'o fishes that were Hina's brothers. And it was in this way that the Great Flood came to Hawaii.

And after the waters of the Ocean had gone back to their own place, Koni-konia the King, with Hina and his people, went back to the place where their houses had been. All was washed away; there were mud and sand where their houses and fields had been. Soon the sun dried up the puddles and the wetness in the ground; growth came again; they built their houses and cultivated their fields; and Koni-konia, with Hina and with his people, lived once again in a wide land beside the Great Ocean.

HINA, THE WOMAN IN THE MOON

A WEARY woman was Hina, and as the years grew on her she grew more and more weary. All day she sat outside her house beating out tapas for clothes for her family, making cloths out of the bark of a tree by beating it on a board with a mallet. Weary indeed was Hina with making tapas all the day outside her house. And when she might see no more to beat out the tapas, she would have to get her gourd and bring water to the house. Often she would stumble in the dark, coming back with her gourd of water. There was no one in her house to help her. Her son went sailing from island to island, robbing people, and her daughter went to live with the wild people in the forest. Her husband had become bad tempered, and he was always striving to make her do more and more work.

As Hina grew old she longed more and more to go to a place where she might sit and rest herself. And one day, when she was given a new task and was sent to fish up shrimps amongst the rocks with a net, she cried out, "Oh, that I might go away from this place, and to a place where I might stay and rest myself."

The Rainbow heard Hina and had pity on her. It made an arching path for her from the rocks up to the heavens. With the net in her hands she went along that path. She thought she would go up to the heavens and then over to the Sun, and that she would go into the Sun and rest herself there.

She went higher and higher along the arch of the Rainbow. But as she went on, the rays of the Sun beat on her more and more strongly. She held the net over her head and went on and on. But when she went beyond the clouds and there was nothing to shelter her, the rays of the Sun burnt her terribly. On and on she went, but as she went higher she could only crawl along the path. Then the fire of the Sun's rays began to torture her and shrivel her. She could go no farther, and, slipping back along the Rainbow arch, she came to earth again.

It was dark now. She stood outside her house and saw her husband coming back from the pool with a gourd of water, stumbling and saying ill-tempered words about her. And when she showed herself to him he scolded because she had not been there to bring the water to the house.

Now that the Sun was gone down and his rays were no longer upon her, her strength came back to Hina. She looked up into the sky, and she saw the full Moon there, and she said: "To the Moon I will go. It is very quiet, and there I can sit for a long, long time and rest myself."

But first she went into the house for the calabash that held all the things that on earth were precious to her. She came out of her house carrying the calabash, and there before her door was a moon-rainbow.

Her husband came and asked her where she was going; because she carried her calabash he knew she was going far. "I am going to the Moon, to a place where I can rest myself," she said. She began to climb along the arch of the Rainbow. And now she was almost out of her husband's reach. But he sprang up and caught her foot in his hand. He fell back, twisting and breaking her foot as he fell.

But Hina went on. She was lamed, and she was filled with pain; and yet she rejoiced as she went along through the quiet night. On and on she went. She came to where the Stars were, and she said incantations to them, that they might show her how to come to the Moon. And the Stars showed her the way, and she came at last to the Moon.

She came to the Moon with the calabash that had her precious possessions; and the Moon gave her a place where she might rest.

There Hina stayed. And the people of Hawaii can look up to the bright Moon and see her there. She sits, her foot lamed, and with her calabash by her side. Seeing her there, the people call her, not "Hina" any more, but "Lono Moku"—that is, "Lame Lono." And standing outside the door you can see her now—Hina, the Woman in the Moon. But some say that, instead of the calabash, she took with her her tapa board and mallet; and they say that the fine fleecy clouds that you see around the Moon are really the fine tapa cloths that Hina beats out.

THE TWO GREAT BROTHERS

NI-HE-U AND KANA

How Ni-he-u and Kana Won Their Mother Back.

KANA and Ni-he-u were brothers. Ni-he-u was such a
great warrior that he could fight against a whole army
without thinking about the odds, and he was able to
carry such a war club that, by resting one end of it in his canoe
and putting the other end against a cliff, he could walk from the
canoe on to the land. Certainly an extraordinary man was
Ni-he-u.

But if Ni-he-u was extraordinary, Kana was many times
more extraordinary. And what an extraordinary life Kana had!
When he was born he was in the form of a piece of rope—just
a piece of rope! But his grandmother (Uli was her name) took
him to her house and reared him. As he began to grow he had to
have a special house built for him; it had to be a very long

house, a house that had to be lengthened out as Kana kept growing. At last the house that Kana lived in stretched from the mountains to the edge of the sea.

The name of the mother of Ni-he-u and Kana was Hina. She was carried away from her husband, the boys' father. When Ni-he-u heard that his mother had been carried off he went to his father and said: "Neither I nor you can get to her and bring her back. Only Kana, my brother, can do that. You must go to him yourself, my father, and ask him to do it. Don't be afraid of him and run away if he should turn and look at you. Just keep your eyes away from him, and then you won't be frightened." After Ni-he-u had told him this, the Chief, his father, went off to find Kana.

When he came to where he was living, Kana looked at him, and the sight of Kana was so terrible that his father turned round and would have run away. But Kana called to him and said, "What have you come for?" "I have come to tell you that the mother of you two has been carried off by Pe-pe'e, the Chief of the Hill of Hau-pu, and she is now in Mo-lo-kai, and unless you, Kana, go to bring her back, no one can bring her back."

When Kana heard this, he said, "Go and call all your people together and order them to hew out a canoe by which we can get to Mo-lo-kai." The Chief then went back, and he sent out an order to his people: they should gather together and hew out a great double canoe that would be ten fathoms in length. His people did as they were ordered. Then they thought that all was ready for the voyage to Mo-lo-kai.

But when the double canoe was brought down to where Kana was, he just stretched out his hand and laid it on it, and the canoe sank out of sight. Other canoes of the same length were hollowed out. But Kana did the same thing to them: he laid his hand on one after another of them, and one after another they all sank down into the sea. His father and the men of the island were without a canoe in which to make the voyage to Mo-lo-kai.

When the Chief told this to Ni-he-u, his son answered him: "Then the only thing to do is to go to Uli, my grandmother and Kana's grandmother, and ask her what to do." The Chief went to her. And when he came before Uli, she said, "There is only one canoe that Kana can travel in; it is in Pali-uli, and it is buried there. Go, get all your people together and send them off to get that canoe." And Uli chanted:

"Go, get it,
Go, get it,
Go, get the canoe:
The canoe that is covered with the cloak of the old woman;
The canoe that jumps playfully in the calm;
The canoe that rises and eats the cords that bind it:
Go, get it,
Go, get it,
Go, get the canoe."

She told the Chief where to dig and how to dig for the canoe that would bring Kana to Mo-lo-kai.

So he took his men to Pali-uli, and there they all began to dig. The men thought that their labor would be in vain, for they never expected they would come by a canoe by digging for it. They worked in the rain and under the thunder and lightning. And when they had dug for the whole length of a day they came, first on the sticks of the bow and stern of the canoe, and then the body of it. It was a great double canoe. With much labor it was dragged down to the sea.

Then Ni-he-u and Kana made ready to go aboard it and to sail over to Mo-lo-kai. But their mother's captor prepared against their coming. He sent the plover, Ko-lea, and the wandering tattler, Uli-li, to fly around and look for Kana and Ni-he-u. And he told them to go also to the warrior who guarded the ocean ways for him, Ke-au-lei-ne-kahi the Swordfish, and command him to pierce the canoe that was on its way, and to slay Ni-he-u and Kana.

Kana and Ni-he-u were on their way to Mo-lo-kai. When they boarded the canoe, Kana folded himself into many folds, but for all his foldings he took up the whole length of the canoe. When they were halfway across they were met by Ke-au-lei-ne-kahi the Swordfish. He smote the canoe with the sword that was in his snout. Then Ni-he-u stood up, and with his war club he struck at the Swordfish. He killed Ke-au-lei-ne-kahi there and then, and after that there was no one to guard the seas and prevent their crossing.

So they came to Mo-lo-kai and saw the hill Hau-pu. Then Ni-he-u started toward it. He wanted to go by himself to the top of Hau-pu and rescue his mother all alone. Around the house that was on the top of the hill was a fence of thick and wide leaves—they were thick enough and wide enough to keep the high wind from the Chief's house. When Ni-he-u came up to this fence he began to beat the leaves down with his great war club. Then the wind struck the house. "What has caused the wind to blow upon us?" said Pe-pe'e, Hina's captor. "There is a boy outside with a club; he has beaten down your fence," said his watchman. "It is Ni-he-u, my brave son. He is without fear," said Hina.

Then Ni-he-u came in. He took hold of his mother and started to carry her down the side of the hill. And as they were going Hina said, very foolishly: "What great strength you have, my brave son! And who would have known that all your strength is in the strands of your hair?" Ko-lea and Uli-li heard what she said. They flew after Ni-he-u and his mother; they flew down and they grabbed Ni-he-u by the hair.

He had to put Hina down while he took up his club and fought with the birds. They were drawing his strength away so that he could hardly carry his great club as they pulled out of his head the strands of his hair. He struck at Ko-lea and Uli-li.

But while he was striking at them, Hina, frightened, ran back to the Chief's house.

When Ni-he-u came to the canoe he was questioned by his brother. "Where is our mother?" "I had taken her; we were on our way when I was attacked by birds. I had to lay her down; then she was frightened; she ran back and I could not go to fetch her again." "You stay and watch in the canoe while I go to get our mother," Kana said.

Kana stood by the hill on which was the Chief's house and rose above it. He stretched himself until he was up in the blue of the sky. But the hill rose up too. Kana had to stretch and stretch himself. And as he stretched himself he became thinner and thinner. Then all that Ni-he-u could see of his brother was a pair of legs. He saw them growing thinner and thinner as the hill went up and Kana went up. But nothing happened except that the hill and the man kept rising higher and higher. Then after three days, Ni-he-u became angry, and he made a cut in one of Kana's legs.

It was three days more before the numbness of this cut reached up to Kana's head. At last it came to him, and he stooped over the sea and over the mountain and reached to Kona, and put his head down at his grandmother's door and asked what was the meaning of the numbness that had come on one of his legs. His grandmother told him it was because his brother had got tired and wanted to remind him that he was waiting for him to bring his mother back. "But what am I to do?" Kana asked. "The hill keeps rising and rising."

Then said his grandmother: "The hill keeps towering up, but if you rise above it, and then stoop over and break off the flipper on the right side—for the hill is really a turtle—and after that stoop over and break off the flipper on the left side, it will not be able to rise up any more, and you will then be able to conquer it."

When he heard that said, Kana rose up once more. He towered over the hill Hau-pu. He stooped over, reached down, and he broke off the flipper that was on the right side. Again he stooped over, and he broke off the flipper that was on the left side. And when these two flippers were broken off the power went out of Hau-pu. It rose no more. Then Kana stepped on the hill, and it broke to pieces. The pieces fell into the sea. They were left there in the shape of rocks and little islets. And that is all that is left of the hill Hau-pu.

Then Kana and Ni-he-u took back their mother in the canoe, and she lived ever afterward with her own husband in her own house. But Kana did not live there. He went to stretch himself in the long house that went from the mountains to the edge of the sea.

How Kana and Ni-he-u Brought Back the Sun and Moon and Stars after They Had Been Taken Away.

ONCE the Sun and Moon and Stars were taken away; they were taken away by Ka-hoa-alii, and the people of the world would have been left in cold and darkness if Kana and his brother Ni-he-u had not gone to find them and bring them back.

This story begins with Ni-he-u. Once when he was crossing the island of Hawaii he heard about Ka-hoa-alii's man: he was of tremendous size and he kept the people fishing and cooking for him so that they had no time nor strength to do anything for themselves. The people were pitying themselves and complaining when Ni-he-u came amongst them.

Then Ni-he-u saw that man of tremendous size, and he flung his club at him; the stroke of the great club knocked Ka-hoa-alii's man over. And after he had flung his club Ni-he-u went on to his grandmother's house. He told her what he had done. She was made afraid, and she told him that trouble would come because of his mischief. "Go," she said, "and find your brother Kana, and bring him here to us, for we shall need his help."

But before he went Uli made him help her fix a long rope that she had. She took the rope and she tied it to the post of her house, and she brought the end of it down to the seashore, and she tied it to a great stone there. The people wondered, and Ni-he-u wondered at what Uli did. Then Ni-he-u went off to find his brother Kana.

Meanwhile Ka-hoa-alii had heard what Uli's grandson had done to his man. "I will punish Ni-he-u for this, and I will punish all the people of Hawaii," he said. "Now I will take away the Sun and the Moon and the Stars from their sky. I will leave the people in cold and darkness; only where I am will there be warmth and light."

Ni-he-u found his brother, and he started with him for their grandmother's house. While they were on their way the darkness came, for the Sun was taken out of the sky suddenly. But as they went on they struck against the rope that Uli had stretched from the post of her house to the stone on the seashore. Holding the rope, they came to the house. Kana did not go within, for no house was high enough to hold him. The two of them saw their grandmother seated by a blazing fire with lights all around her.

"So you have come," said their grandmother to them. "You are the only two in all the world that can bring the Sun and the Moon and the Stars back into our sky. Ka-hoa-alii has taken them away, and you must go to where Ka-hoa-alii is. Before I tell you what to do, do you, Kana, stretch yourself upwards, and see if there is any light in the sky."

Kana stretched himself upwards until his head was near the sky. He looked around, and he saw a little light in it. He brought himself down again, and he told his grandmother what he had seen.

Then said Uli: "You, Kana, and you, Ni-he-u, will have to go to the country that Ka-hoa-alii rules over. Go straight toward the place that the sun used to rise in. The fine rain will fall on you and the cold will get into your bones, but go on and on until you come to where an old woman sits at the bottom of a cliff. She is my sister; Luahine-kai-kapu she is named, and she is blind. Tell her that you are Uli's grandchildren, and she will direct you to the country that Ka-hoa-alii rules over."

So Kana and Ni-he-u started off from their grandmother's house. They went in a straight line toward the place that the Sun used to rise in. As they went on the fine rain fell on them and the cold went into their bones. Kana took up Ni-he-u and carried him on. But still the fine rain fell on them and still the cold crept into their bones. Then when they came to the place that is called Kaha-kae-kaea, Ni-he-u lay down to die.

Kana left him wrapped in leaves under a loulu palm and went on. He came to where an old woman sat at the bottom of a cliff; she was blind, and he knew that she was Luahine-kai-kapu, his grandmother's sister.

"Whose child are you?" said Luahine-kai-kapu to Kana. "Your sister's, Uli's grandchild," said Kana. "What have you come for?" said she. "I have come to get the Sun and Moon and Stars that Ka-hoa-alii has taken from our sky; I am the only one who can bring them back. Show me the way to Ka-hoa-alii's country."

"I have no eyes," said Luahine-kai-kapu; "I cannot see to show you the way." "Lie down under this coconut tree," said Kana. Luahine-kai-kapu lay down. Kana picked off the young shoots of the coconut and called out to her, "Luahine-kai-kapu, turn your face toward the sky." She turned her face up as directed; Kana then threw the two young shoots at her eyes.

Then he struck her in the eyes, and she jumped up and cried out with a loud voice, "Oh, I am killed!" Kana then said to her, "Be quiet and rub your eyes." The old woman began rubbing her eyes. After she had done this she cried out that she was able to see as before.

"Before I send you into the country of Ka-hoa-alii, I shall

have to do something to make your hands different," said Lua-hine-kai-kapu. She took ku-kui nut and charcoal and she pounded them together and she made a paste. She rubbed the paste she had made on the great hands of Kana. "Now," said she, "you have hands like the hands of Ka-hoa-alii." Then she told him what to do when he came to the place where Ka-hoa-alii lived.

She set a fire before him to guide him, and she set a wind at his back to help him on. And helped on by the wind and guided by the fire, Kana came at last to the borders of Ka-hoa-alii's country. Then the fire died down, and he had no guide to go before him. But still the wind helped him on.

He came to the place where Ka-hoa-alii was. He hid and watched him. Ka-hoa-alii would lift up a great stone that covered a hole in the sky, and take food up in his hands, and feast with his attendants. And when they had feasted they would go into the house and play games. Thus Ka-hoa-alii and his attendants passed the day; they feasted and they played games, and they played games and they feasted.

Kana did what Luahine-kai-kapu told him to do. He watched all they did. When they had gone into the house he went to the great stone. He lifted it up. He propped it up with his feet. Then he put his two hands down into the hole.

Those below put things into his hands. They were things to eat. Kana flung them away, and put his hands down again. Those below put water into his hands. He emptied the water out. Kana put his hands down again. Those below put birds into his hands; he took them up and let them fly around; they were the birds that cry when darkness is going. Now as they flew around they cried, "Kia-wea, Kia-wea."

He put his hands down again. Now his hands were filled with Stars. He took them up and flung them into the sky. There they stayed—the Stars that we still see. He lowered his hands again.

The Moon was put into his hands. He put the Moon into the blue sky with the Stars, and it stayed there, giving light.

Kana put his hands down again. This time a single bird was put into his hands. He took it up and put it beside him. It was the crowing cock. He put his hands down once more; the warm Sun was put into his hands. He held the bright Sun up. He put it into the sky. The cock beside him crew.

The cock crew, and Ka-hoa-alii, hearing it crow, came out of his house. He saw Kana standing there, and he saw the Sun shining in the sky. He went toward Kana to kill him, but he saw how tall and how strong Kana was, and he was afraid to touch him. And Kana, seeing that Ka-hoa-alii was afraid of him, demanded from him the Water of Life, the Water of Kane, so that he might restore his brother with it. Ka-hoa-alii gave him the Water of Kane.

Kana then went to Kaha-kae-kaea. His brother Ni-he-u was there, wrapped in leaves under the loulu palm. He gave him the Water of Life, and life came back again to Ni-he-u. Afterward Ka-hoa-alii came to where they were. He gave them a canoe made out of white chicken feathers, and in that canoe Kana and Ni-he-u returned to Hawaii. They went to their grandmother's house, and they saw the Sun in the heavens, and the Moon following the Sun, and the Stars with the Moon. And never again were these bright lights taken out of our sky.

AU-KE-LE THE SEEKER

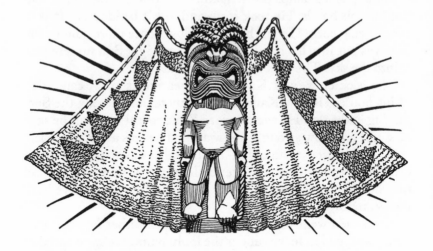

IN a land that is now lost, in Ku-ai-he-lani, the Country that Supports the Heavens, there lived a King whose name was Iku. He had twelve children, and of these eleven grew up without ever having received any favor or any promise from their father.

But when the twelfth child was born—Au-ke-le was his name —his father took him up in his arms, and he promised him all the honor and power and glory that was his, and he promised him the kingship of Ku-ai-he-lani, the Country that Supports the Heavens.

The other children were angry when they saw their father take little Au-ke-le up in his arms, and they were more angry when they heard the promises that were made to him. And the eldest brother, who was the angriest of all, said, "I am the eldest born, and my father never made such promises to me, and he never took me up in his arms and fondled me." And this brother, who was now a man grown, went from before his father, and his other brothers went with him.

Au-ke-le grew up. His father gave him many of his possessions—feather cloaks, and whale-tooth necklaces, and many sharp and polished weapons. He grew up to be the handsomest of handsome youths, with a body that was straight and faultless. One day, knowing that they had gone to play games in a certain house, he went to follow his brothers. But Iku, his father, said to him, "Do not go where your brothers have gone; they are angry with you, and they have always been angry with you, and it may be that they will do some harm to you in that place." But in spite of the words of his father Au-ke-le followed his brothers. He came to the house where his brothers were, and he shot his arrow into it. One of his brothers took up the arrow and said, "This is not a stranger's arrow; this is an arrow from our own house; see, it is twisted." The eldest brother, who was the angriest of all, took up the arrow and broke it to pieces. He sent the others outside to invite Au-ke-le within the house. And Au-ke-le, believing in the kindness of his brothers, and thinking they were going to let him join in their games, came within.

But they had made a plan against him. They laid hold upon him when he came within the house, and, at the words of the eldest brother, they uncovered a pit and they flung Au-ke-le down into it.

In that pit there lived a mo-o whose name was Ka-mo'o-i-na-nea. This mo-o was really Au-ke-le's grandmother. She had been a mortal woman; but she had transformed herself into a mo-o, and now she lived in that pit, and she devoured any creature that came into it.

The angry brother called out, "Mo-o, Mo-o, here is your food; eat it." Then he went away. But a younger brother who felt kindly to Au-ke-le whispered down, "Do not eat this youth, Mo-o, for he is your own grandson." The mo-o heard the words of both. She came before Au-ke-le and she signed for him to follow her. He followed, and they came out on the dry sand that was before the ocean.

Then the mo-o spoke to Au-ke-le her grandson. "There is a land beyond this sea," she said, "a land that I traveled through in my young days before I took on this dragon form. Very few people live in that land. You must sail to it; living there you will become great and wise.

"The name of that land is Ka-la-ke'e-nui-a-Kane. The mountains are so high that the stars rest upon them. The people who live there are Na-maka-o-Kahai, the Queen, and her four brothers, who take the forms of birds, and two women servants. The watchers of her land are a dog called Mo-e-la and a great and fierce bird called Ha-lu-lu.

"I will give you things to take with you. Here is a calabash that has a Magic in it. It has an ax in it also that you can use. And here is food that will last for the longest voyage. It is a leaf, but if you put it to your lips it will take away your hunger and your thirst. I give you my skirt of feathers also; the touch of it will bring death to your enemies." Then his mo-o grandmother left him, and Au-ke-le was upon the seashore with a calabash that had Magic in it, with the leaves that stayed his hunger and his thirst, and with the skirt of feathers that would destroy his enemies. And he had in his heart the resolve to go to the land that his mo-o grandmother had told him about.

In the meantime Iku-mai-lani, the kind brother, had gone back to his father's house. Iku asked what had happened to his favorite son. Then Iku-mai-lani, weeping, told his father that the boy had been flung into the pit where the mo-o was and that he feared the mo-o had devoured him as she had devoured others. Then the father and mother of Au-ke-le wept.

As they were weeping he came within the house. His mother and father rejoiced over him, and Iku-mai-lani hurried to give the news to his brothers. They were building a canoe, and when the eldest brother heard of Au-ke-le's escape, and heard the sound of rejoicing in his father's house, he gave orders to have all preparations made for sailing and to have the food cooked and everyone aboard, that they might sail at once from the land.

It was then that Au-ke-le came up to where they were. He called out to his kind brother, to Iku-mai-lani, and asked him what he might do to be let go in the canoe with them. His brother said: "How can we take you when it is on your account only that we are going away from the country we were born in? We are going because you only of all of us have been promised the kingdom and the glory that belongs to our father. And we are going because we tried to kill you, and now are ashamed of what we did."

Still Au-ke-le craved to be let go with them. Then the kind brother said to him: "You cannot gain your way through us. But with our eldest brother is a boy—a little son whom he is taking along, and for whom he has a great love. If the child of our eldest brother should ask you to come on board you will surely be let come."

Then Au-ke-le went to the canoe. And the little boy who was his eldest brother's son saw him and clapped his hands and called out to him, "My uncle, come on board of the ship and be one of us."

Au-ke-le then went on board. The eldest brother, he who had been the most angry with him, let Au-ke-le stay because his young son had brought him on board. Au-ke-le then sent the men back to his father's house for the things that his grandmother had given him—for the calabash with the Magic in it, and for the feather dress. The men brought these things to him; then the paddlers took up their paddles; the canoe went into the deep sea, and Au-ke-le and his brothers departed from the land of Ku-ai-he-lani, the Country that Supports the Heavens.

They sailed far and far away, and no land came to their sight. All the food they had brought in the canoe was eaten, and they no longer had food or drink. Their men died of hunger and thirst. Au-ke-le's brothers went below, and they stayed in the bottom of the canoe, for they were waiting for death to come to them.

At last the boy who was the son of the eldest brother went down to seek his father. He was lying there, too weak to move by reason of his hunger and thirst. And Au-ke-le's eldest brother said to his son: "How pitiful it is for you, my son! For my own life I have no regret, for I have been many days in the world; but I weep for you, who have lived so short a time and have but so short a time to live. Here is all I have to give you—a joint of sugarcane." Then the boy replied, "I have no need for food— my uncle Au-ke-le has a certain leaf which he puts to my lips, and with that leaf my hunger and my thirst are satisfied." His father hardly heard what he said, so weak he had become. Then the boy went back to Au-ke-le.

And when he came before his uncle again tears were streaming down his face. "Why do you weep?" Au-ke-le asked. "I am weeping for my father, who is almost dead from hunger." Au-ke-le said: "You too would have died from hunger had I not come with you. I am hated by your father as his most bitter enemy, but I would act as a brother acts. Now let us go to where my brothers are."

So they went below. Au-ke-le went to each of his brothers and put the leaf to their lips. It was as if each of them had got food and drink. Their faintness went from them, and they were able to get about the ship once more.

Soon afterward they came in sight of land; Au-ke-le knew that this was the country that his mo-o grandmother had told him about. And, remembering what he had been told about the dangers of this land, he asked his brothers to let him take charge of the canoe, so that they might avoid these dangers. His brothers said, "Why did you not build a canoe for yourself, so that you might take charge of it and give orders about it?" Au-ke-le said, "If you give me charge of the canoe, we shall be saved; but if you take charge yourselves, we shall be destroyed." His brothers laughed at him.

In a while they saw birds approaching the ship—four birds. Au-ke-le, remembering what his mo-o grandmother had told him, knew that these were the Queen's brothers. They came and lit on the yards, and asked of those below what they had come for. Au-ke-le told his brothers to say that they had not come to make war and that they had come on a voyage of sight-seeing. His brothers would not say this; instead they cried out to the birds, "Ours is a ship to make war." The birds flew back; they told their sister Na-maka that the ship had come to make war. Then the Queen put on her war skirt and went down to the shore.

Au-ke-le knew that all in the canoe would be destroyed. He took up his calabash that had the Magic in it, and he threw it into the sea. As he did this he saw the Queen standing there with her war skirt on. She took up her feathered standard and shook it in the air. Au-ke-le sprang from the ship and swam after the floating calabash. Then the ship and all who were on it disappeared: Na-maka the Queen made a sign, and they were seen no more.

And now Au-ke-le was left on the land that his grandmother had told him about—the land of Ka-la-ke'e-nui-a-Kane, where the stars rest on the tops of the mountains. He brought the calabash that had his Magic in it and the skirt of feathers that his mo-o grandmother had given him, and he rested under a tree by the seashore.

The dog that was called Mo-e-la, the Day Sleeper, smelt his blood and barked. And, hearing her dog bark, Na-maka the Queen came out of her house and called to her four bird brothers: "You must go and find out what man of flesh and blood my dog is barking at." But her four brothers, being sleepy, said,

"Send your two women servants and let us rest." So the Queen sent her two women servants to find out what the dog was barking at. "And if it be a creature of flesh and blood, kill him," said the Queen.

Then the two servants went toward the shore where Au-ke-le was resting. But his Magic told him what was coming and what he should do. "When they come you must call the servants by their names, and they will be so abashed at a stranger's knowing them that they will not know what to do."

So when the Queen's two women servants came before him Au-ke-le called out, "It is U-po-ho and it is Hua-pua-i-na-nea." The two servants were so abashed because their names were known to this stranger that they stood there looking at each other.

Then Au-ke-le called them to him, and they came, and they sat near him. He asked them to play the game that is played with black and white stones. He moved the stones, and as he moved them he chanted, and his chant was to let them know who he was.

> "This is my turn; your turn now;
> Now we pause; the blacks cannot win;
> The whites have won:
> Nothing can break the boy from Ku-ai-he-lani."

The servants knew then that he was from Ku-ai-he-lani, the Country that Supports the Heavens. They said to him, "We were sent to kill you, but we are going back to tell the Queen that in no place could we find a creature of flesh and blood."

They returned, and they told the Queen that neither on the uplands nor on the seashore, neither on the tops of the trees nor on the tops of the cliffs, were they able to find a creature of flesh and blood. While they were speaking the Queen's dog came out and barked again. Her four bird brothers had rested, and the

Queen sent them to search for the creature of flesh and blood that the dog had barked at.

Then the Magic in his calabash spoke again to Au-ke-le. "Four birds are coming toward you. You must greet them and you must call them by their names. They will be so abashed at their names being known to a stranger that they will not know what to do."

As the four birds came toward him Au-ke-le called aloud: "This is Ka-ne-mo-e, and I give greetings to him. This is Ka-ne-a-pua, and I give greetings to him. This is Le-a-pua, and I give greetings to him. And this is Ka-hau-mana." The four bird brothers were amazed to hear their names spoken by a stranger, and they said to each other, "What can we do with this man who knows our names, even?" And another said, "He can take our lives from us." And they spoke to each other again and said, "We have one thing worthy to give to this man: let us give him our sister, the Queen."

So the four brothers came to Au-ke-le, and they offered him the Queen to be his wife. Au-ke-le was pleased; he told them that he would go to the Queen's house.

The four bird brothers went back to tell the Queen about the man who was coming to her and to whom they had promised her. The Queen said, "If he is such that he can overcome the dangers that are before him, I will marry him, and he will be the ruler with me of the land of Ka-la-ke'e-nui-a-Kane."

When the brothers had gone his Magic spoke again to Au-ke-le, and it said: "When you go to the Queen, don't enter the house at once, for that would mean your death. If they offer you food in a calabash, don't eat it, for that would mean your death. The dog that is called Mo-e-la will be set upon you, and if you overcome him the four brothers will attack you. Eat the melons on the vines outside the house, and they will be meat and drink for you."

After hearing the words that his Magic had said to him,

Au-ke-le went to the house of the Queen. He stood outside the door, and as he stood there the Queen said to her women servants, "Use your powers now and destroy this creature of flesh and blood." But when the servants saw the man who knew their names, one changed herself into a rat and ran into a hole, and the other changed herself into a lizard and ran up a tree.

Then Mo-e-la the dog came toward him; he opened his mouth wide and he showed all his teeth. But when he was touched by the skirt that Au-ke-le had been given, the dog was turned into ashes. And then the Queen, on seeing the death of her watchdog, bowed down her head and wept.

She called upon her brothers to kill the stranger. But they were abashed at his knowing their names, and they wanted to hide from him. One turned himself into a rock and lay by the doorway, and another turned himself into a log of wood and lay beside his brother, and the third changed himself into a coral reef, and the fourth became a pool of water.

Food was brought to Au-ke-le, but he would eat none of it. He went to the vine, and he ate the melons that were growing there, and he found that the melons gave food and drink to him. And when the Queen and her brothers saw him eating the melons they said to each other: "How wonderful this man is! He is eating the food that we eat. Who could have told him where to find it?" After that he won the Queen, and she became his wife.

But it was after his adventure with the bird Ha-lu-lu that Au-ke-le knew that the Queen had come to love him and was inclined to be kind to him. One day he was standing by the seashore, looking out to the place where the canoe that had had his brothers on board was sunk, when a great shadow came over where he was and covered the light of the sun. He looked up, and he saw above him the outstretched wings of a great bird.

Immediately he picked up the calabash that had his Magic in it; then the bird Ha-lu-lu seized him and flew off with him.

The bird flew to a cave that was in the face of a great high cliff. He stowed Au-ke-le there. And Au-ke-le, searching the cave, found two men who had been carried off by Ha-lu-lu, the great bird. "We are two that are to be devoured," said the men. "What does the bird do when she comes to devour us?" said Au-ke-le. "She stretches her right wing into the cave and draws out a man. She devours him. Then she stretches her left wing into the cave and draws out another man." "Is the cave deep?" Au-ke-le asked. "It is deep," said the men. "Go, then," said Au-ke-le, "and make a fire in the depth of the cave."

The men did this. Then Au-ke-le opened the calabash that his mo-o grandmother had given him, and he took out the ax that was in it. He waited for the giant bird to stretch her wing within. When she did he cut the wing off with his ax, and the two men took it and threw the wing on the fire. The other wing reached in; Au-ke-le cut off the other wing, too. Then the beak was stuck in, and Au-ke-le cut off head and beak.

After Ha-lu-lu the great bird had been killed, Au-ke-le took the feathers from her head and threw them over the cliff. The feathers flew on until they came to where the Queen was. She saw them, and she knew them for the head feathers of the bird Ha-lu-lu, and she cried when she saw them.

When her brothers came to her she said, "Here are the head feathers of the bird Ha-lu-lu, and now there is no great bird to guard the island." But her brothers said, "It is right that Ha-lu-lu should be killed, for she devoured men." They waited then to see what their sister would do to Au-ke-le, who was in the cave. She brought the rainbow, the short-ended rainbow that has only three colors, red, yellow, and green, and she set it against the cliff. And by the bridge of the rainbow Au-ke-le was able to get down from the cliff.

When his wife and her brothers saw him come back they welcomed Au-ke-le with joy. The Queen gave him everything that was at her command. And she sent a message to her uncles, who were in the sky, to tell them that she had given her husband all her possessions—the things that were above and below, that were on the uplands and on the lowlands, the drift iron, the iron that stands in the ground, the whale's tooth, the turtle-shell, the things that grow on the land, and the cluster of stars. All these things were his now. But with all these things in his possession Au-ke-le was not satisfied, for he thought upon the canoe that was sunken and on his brothers who were all drowned.

He dreamed of his brothers and of his young nephew; and, with the thoughts that he had, he could not enjoy himself on the land that he ruled over. And, seeing her husband so sad, sorrow for him entered the heart of the Queen. He told her that he thought of the men who had come with him and who were now dead. And when he spoke of what was in his mind the Queen said: "If you have great strength and courage, your brothers may come back to life again; but if your strength or your courage fail, they will never be restored to life, and your own life, perhaps, will be lost." Then Au-ke-le said to the Queen, "What is it that I must do to win them back to life?" And the Queen said: "You must use all your strength and your courage to gain the Water of Everlasting Life, the Water of Ka-ne. If you are able to gain it and bring it to them, your brothers and your nephew will live again." When Au-ke-le heard this from the Queen he ceased to be sorrowful; he ate and he drank, and he had gladness in his possessions. Then he said to the Queen, "What way must I take to gain the Water of Everlasting Life, the Water of Ka-ne?" His wife said: "I will show you the way: from the place where we are standing you must go toward the rising sun, never turning from the road that I set you on. And at the end of your journey you will come to the place where you will find the Water of Everlasting Life, the Water of Ka-ne."

When Au-ke-le heard this he put on his skirt of feathers that his mo-o grandmother had given him; he took up the calabash that had his Magic in it; he kissed his wife farewell; and he took the path from his house that went straight toward the rising sun.

After he had been on his way for a month the Queen came to the door of her house, and she looked toward where he had gone. She saw him, and he was still upon his way. At the end of another month she went out again and looked toward where he had gone. He was still upon the path that led to the rising sun. Another month passed, and she went and looked toward where he had gone. No trace of her husband could she see, and she knew that he must have gone off the path she had shown him. She began to weep, and when her four brothers came before her she said, "Your brother-in-law has fallen into space, and he is lost."

She then sent her brothers to bring all things and creatures together that they might all mourn for Au-ke-le. They went and they brought the night and the day, the sun, the stars, the thunder, the rainbow, the lightning, the waterspout, the mist, the fine rain. And the grandfather of the Queen, Kau-kihi-ka-malama, who is the Man in the Moon, was sent for, too.

But where indeed was Au-ke-le?

He had left the straight line toward the rising sun; he had fallen into space, and now he was growing weaker and weaker as he fell. But he still had the calabash that had his Magic in it. He held it under his arm; and now he spoke and asked where they were. His Magic said to him: "We have gone outside the line that was shown to us, and now I think that we shall never get back. There is nothing in the sky to help us or to show us the way; all that was in the sky has gone down to the earth—the night and the day, the sun and the stars, the thunder, the rainbow, the lightning, the waterspout, the mist, the fine rain. No, I can see no thing and no creature that can help us." Au-ke-le asked, "Who is it that is still up there?" His Magic replied: "Go straight and lay hold upon him, and we may be saved. That is Kau-kihi-ka-malama, the Man in the Moon."

The reason that Kau-kihi-ka-malama had not gone down to earth with the others was that he had delayed to prepare food to bring down to the earth, for he thought that there was no food there. He was just starting off when Au-ke-le came up to him and held him tightly. "Whose conceited child are you?" the Man in the Moon asked. "My back has never been climbed, even by my own granddaughter, and now you come here and climb over it. Whose conceited child are you?" "Yours," said Au-ke-le. "I will take you to earth, and my granddaughter Na-maka will tell me who you are." And so Kau-kihi-ka-malama brought Au-ke-le back to earth. And when he reached the earth all the people there wept with joy to see him. Then the sun, the day, the night, the lightning, the thunder, the mist, the fine rain, the waterspout, and the Man in the Moon all returned back to the heavens.

But nothing would do Au-ke-le but to set out again to find the Water of Everlasting Life, the Water of Ka-ne. So he started off from the door of his house, and he went in a straight line toward the rising sun. And in six months from the time he started he stood by the edge of a hole at the bottom of which was the Water of Everlasting Life, the Water of Ka-ne.

He climbed over the shoulder of the guard, and the guard said to him: "Eh, there! Whose conceited child are you? My back has never been climbed over before, and now you come here and do it. Whose conceited child are you?" "Your own," said Au-ke-le. "My own by whom?" "My father is Iku," said Au-ke-le. "Then you are the grandson of Ka-po-ino and Ka-mo'o-i-na-nea." "I am." "My greetings to you, my lord," said the guardian of the edge of the hole.

Au-ke-le had to go deep down into the hole to get the Water of Everlasting Life, the Water of Ka-ne. The guardian of the edge of the hole warned him that he must not strike the bamboo that was growing on one side, because if he did the sound would reach the ears of one who would cover up the water. Au-ke-le went down. He came to a second guardian, and he made himself known to him, claiming relationship with him through Ka-mo'o-i-na-nea, his mo-o grandmother. This guardian told him to go on, but he warned him not to fall into the lama trees that were growing on one side, for if he did the sound would reach the ears of one who would cover up the Water of Everlasting Life, the Water of Ka-ne.

He went on, and he came to the third guardian, and he made himself known to him, claiming relationship with him through his mo-o grandmother. This guardian told him to keep on his way, but he warned him, above all things, not to fall into the loula palms, for if he did the sound would reach one who would cover up the Water of Everlasting Life, the Water of Ka-ne.

At last he came before the fourth guardian. "Who are you?" he was asked. "The child of Iku." "What has brought you here?" he was asked. "To gain the Water of Everlasting Life, the Water of Ka-ne." "You shall get it. Go to your grandaunt who is at the base of the cliff. She is the Old Woman of the Forbidden Sea. She is blind. You will find her roasting bananas. When she reaches out to take one to eat, you take it and eat it. Do this until all the bananas have been taken from her. When she says, 'What mischievous fellow has come here?' take up the ashes and sprinkle them on her right side, and then climb into her lap."

Au-ke-le kept going and ever going until he came to where his grandaunt sat, roasting bananas—his grandaunt, the Old Woman by the Forbidden Sea. He took the bananas that she was about to eat; he sprinkled her with ashes on her right side, and he climbed into her lap. "Whose conceited child are you?" said the blind old woman. "Your own," said Au-ke-le. "My own through whom?" "Your own through Iku." When his grandaunt heard him say this she asked him what he had come for. He told her he had come for the Water of Everlasting Life, the Water of Ka-ne.

Then the Old Woman by the Forbidden Sea made up a plan by which he might get the water. Ka-hoa-alii, he who watched above the water, had hands that were all black, and no hands but his were permitted to take up the Water of Ka-ne. His grandaunt made Au-ke-le's hands black, and she showed him where to go to come to the water.

Au-ke-le went there. He put down his blackened hands, and the guards gave him a gourd of water. But this, as he had been told by the Old Woman by the Forbidden Sea, was bitter water, and not the Water of Everlasting Life. He threw the water out. He reached his hands down again; and this time the Water of Ka-ne was put into his hands, the Water of Everlasting Life.

He took the gourd into his hands, and he ran back. But he fell into loula palms as he ran on, and the sound came to the ears of Ka-hoa-alii, who was the guardian of the water. Ka-hoa-alii listened, but it was two months before another sound came to him. That was when Au-ke-le got entangled in the lama trees that grew on the side of the hole that he had to travel up. Ka-hoa-alii kept awake and listened. But no sound came to him for two months more. Then he heard the rustling of the bamboo trees that Au-ke-le had fallen into. He came in pursuit. But now Au-ke-le was out of the hole and was flying toward the earth. Ka-hoa-alii followed; but when he asked the watcher how long it was since one had passed that way, he was told that a year and six months had gone by since one came up through the hole. Ka-hoa-alii could not catch up with one who by this time had gone so far; and Au-ke-le, with the Water of Everlasting Life, the Water of Ka-ne, came back to the earth.

He came to where his brothers and his nephew were drowned in the sea, and he poured half of the Water of Ka-ne into the sea. Nothing came up from the sea, and Au-ke-le sat there weeping. Then his wife came to him, and she blamed him for pouring so much of the water into the sea. Out of what was left she took water in her hands and poured it over the sea. Then Au-ke-le looked. In a while there stood a canoe with men climbing the masts, and folding the sails, and coiling the ropes. They were his brothers. Au-ke-le greeted them, and his brothers knew him, and they came to the land.

Then Au-ke-le gave his brothers all his possessions. But they were not satisfied to live on that land with him, and after a while they sailed away for other lands.

Then after long years Au-ke-le said to his wife: "My wife, we have lived long together; I would not die in a foreign land, and I beg that you will let me go so that I may see Ku-ai-he-lani, the country of my parents."

He went, with his wife's four brothers. And they went by a course that brought them there in two days and two nights. Upon their arrival Au-ke-le looked over the land; but he saw no people, and the sound of birds singing or of cocks crowing did not come to him, and then he saw that the land of Ku-ai-he-lani was all grown over with weeds.

He came to the mouth of the cave where his mo-o grandmother used to be. He shouted down to her, but no sound came back from her to him. He went down. The coral of the floor of the sea had grown over her, and she was not able to answer the call of her grandson Au-ke-le.

He broke away the pieces of coral that were around her. He saw the body of his mo-o grandmother, and it was reduced to a thread, almost. He called her name, "Ka-mo'o-i-na-nea."

Ka-mo'o-i-na-nea said "Yes," and she looked up and saw her grandson. She greeted him and asked him what had brought him to her. "I came to see you," he said, "and to ask you where are Iku and the others."

"Iku fought with Ma-ku-o-ae," his grandmother told him. When she said that, Au-ke-le knew that Death and his father had met.

KAULU

THE WORLD'S STRONGEST BOY

KAULU went in search of the brother who was taken away before he was born; he went in search of his kind brother Ka-eha. And first he went down to the seashore. There he saw a great line of surf striking on the beach. "Surf, are you strong?" said Kaulu. "We are!" said the surf. "What strength have you?" said Kaulu. "We'll tell you," said the surf. Then eight waves struck Kaulu, but they did not knock him over.

Said Kaulu, "Say, Hakau-kahi, my right hand, and Lima-pai-hala, my left hand, are you as strong as this surf?" "I am!" said his right hand, and "I am!" said his left hand. Kaulu then reached down and took up the surf. He broke it into little pieces with his right hand and with his left hand, and that is the reason the surf is small to this day.

Then he came upon the large waves, and he said to them, "Waves, you have no strength; you are only good for making the ocean white." The waves said to him, "We are strong and we are also brave." Then they broke upon Kaulu. He took them in his hands and he broke them into the lengths that you see in the waves to this day.

His brother Ka-eha had been carried up into the land that is in the sky, the land that is called Lewa-nu'u or Lewa-lani. As Kaulu went traveling on to find this place he came to where Lono-ka-eho was standing up. Lono-ka-eho had eight foreheads, and the topmost of his foreheads was touching the sky. "Who is the one with the sharp foreheads?" Kaulu said. "Lono-ka-eho, Lono-ka-eho," said his attendants, "here is one asking your name!" Lono-ka-eho shouted down to Kaulu, "Are you so strong that you want to provoke me to come down to you?" "I have a little strength, but not much," said Kaulu. Lono-ka-eho's foreheads struck down from the heavens. Then said

Kaulu's hands to him, "What are we to do?" "You, Hakau-kahi, my right hand, and you, Lima-pai-hala, my left hand, hold him down."

So when Lono-ka-eho struck down with all his foreheads, Hakau-kahi and Lima-pai-hala, Kaulu's two hands, held them down to the ground until the grasses and the ohia trees grew over them. And there Lono-ka-eho stays to this day, on the hill of Olo-mana.

Then Kaulu went on again. He wanted to get into the blue sky where his brother Ka-eha was. He went on and he came to where the wizard Moko-li'i sat by the wayside.

Now Moko-li'i sat by the wayside to devour every man and woman who came that way. "Where are you going?" said Moko-li'i to Kaulu when he came along. "I am going up into the blue sky," said Kaulu; "will you take me up, Moko-li'i?" "I will take you up, and you will become my food for this day." "And you can have me if you are strong," said Kaulu.

The wizard took him in his teeth and carried him up into the blue sky. Then Kaulu commanded his two hands to take hold of Moko-li'i and throw him down on the ground. This his two hands did. Moko-li'i fell down on the ground, where he broke every bone in his body. And where he fell he lies to this day.

And now that he was in the blue sky, Kaulu went through Lewa-nu'u or Lewa-lani looking for his brother. The dwellers in this country knew that Kaulu, the world's strongest boy, had come to look for his brother, and they thought that if Kaulu and Ka-eha came together they would rule the whole of the land. So they tempted Ka-eha to go to ride the surf with them. But before they went down to the surf the dwellers in Lewa-nu'u or Lewa-lani told the King of the Sharks, Ka-la-ke'e-nui, to be there and to devour Ka-eha.

And so when Ka-eha went out on the surf he came into the presence of Ka-la-ke'e-nui. The shark swallowed him up whole. It was just then that Kaulu came into Lewa-nu'u or Lewa-lani; none of the dwellers would tell him where his brother was.

So he went to Maka-li'i, the King of that country. Maka-li'i was sleeping with his face turned up; a very old man he was, the oldest and the most cunning in the land. Maka-li'i's brother was guarding his sleep, and he took up a great rock to fling at Kaulu. Kaulu put up his forefinger and held the rock back. "Oh, look," he said, "here's the rock of the strong man being held back! When is it to fall down?" Maka-li'i's brother then ran off and left Kaulu there.

Kaulu pinched Maka-li'i, and the ancient one wakened up. "Tell me," said Kaulu, "where my elder brother is." "Your elder brother," said Maka-li'i, "is inside the King of the Sharks." "And how shall I come to the King of the Sharks?" "He is in the great mound of coral—the mound that has an opening at the top. People think that this is a mound of coral, but it is really a shark."

So Kaulu went to where Ka-la-ke'e-nui was. "Have you seen my brother?" he said. "Yes," said Ka-la-ke'e-nui; "he is inside me." "Are you strong?" said Kaulu. "Yes, I am pretty strong," said the shark. "What is your strength?" said Kaulu. "If I open my mouth, my upper jaw can reach the heavens while my lower jaw is scraping the bottom of the sea. You can tell my strength by that." Then Kaulu asked his two hands, "Say, Hakau-kahi and Lima-pai-hala, is he strong?" Kaulu's two hands said, "No, no, he is not really strong."

Kaulu went to where the great shark was. Ka-la-ke'e-nui opened his mouth, and Kaulu stepped within and held the shark's jaws open. He shouted to his brother to come out. Then Ka-eha came out of the shark, and this was the first time that Kaulu had seen his brother. They killed the shark then, and they flung its body up into the sky, and there it is to this day. Then Kaulu and his brother Ka-eha went home. Look! there is Ka-la-ke'e-nui's body: some call it The Fish, and some call it The Milky Way.

SANDALWOOD, *you say, and in your thoughts it chimes*
With Tyre and Sidon; to me it rhymes
With places bare upon Pacific mountains,
With spaces empty in the minds of men.

Sandalwood!
The Kings of Hawaii call out their men,
The men go up the mountains in files;
Hands that knew only the stone ax now wield the iron ax:
The Sandalwood trees go down.

More sandalwood is called for:
The men who hunt the whale will buy sandalwood;
The Kings would change canoes for ships.
Men come down from the mountains carrying sandalwood on their backs;
More and more men are levied
They go up the mountains in files; they leave their taro patches so that
        famine comes down on the land.

But this sandalwood grows upon other trees, a parasite;
It needs a growing thing to grow upon;
Its seed and its soil are not enough for it!

Too greedy are the Kings;
Too eager are the men who hunt the whale to sail to Canton with fragrant
        wood to make shrines for the Buddhas;
Too sharp is the iron ax!

Nothing will ever bring together again
The spores and the alien sap that nourished them,
The trees and the trees they planted themselves upon:
Like the myths of peoples,
Like the faiths of peoples,
Like the speech of peoples,
Like the ancient creation chants,
The sandalwood is gone!

A fragrance in shrines—
But the trees will never live again!

NOTES

THE PRINCESS OF THE RAINBOW

PUBLISHED by the Smithsonian Institution, 1911–1912, with the title *The Hawaiian Romance of Laieikawai*, with introduction and translation by Martha Warren Beckwith.

"The story was handed down orally from ancient times in the form of a *kaao*, a narrative rehearsed in prose interspersed with song," says Miss Beckwith. It was reshaped by Haleole, an Hawaiian writer, and published, first as a serial in a newspaper and afterward in book form, in the sixties. "Haleole wrote his tale painstakingly, at times dramatically, but for the most part concerned for its historic interest," says Miss Beckwith. "We gather from his own statement and from the breaks in the story that his material may have been collected from different sources." Miss Beckwith's interpretation of the story is as follows:

"An ancestress rears Rainbow in the forests of Puna. Birds bear her upon their wings and serve her with abundance of food prepared without labor, and of their golden feathers her royal house is built; sweet-scented vines and blossoms surround her; mists shroud her when she goes abroad. Earthquake [the Mo'o or great lizard] guards her dwelling, saves Rainbow from Lightning [the devouring dog from Tahiti], who seeks to destroy her, and bears a messenger to fetch Sun-at-high-noon as bridegroom for the beautiful Rainbow. He is of such a divine character that he dwells in the highest heavens. . . . Noonday, like a bird, bears visitors to his gate, and guards of the shade, Moving-cloud and Great-bright-moon—close it to shut out his brightness. The three regions below him are guarded by maternal uncles and by his father. . . . The Sun god comes to earth and bears Rainbow away with him to the heavens, but later he loves her sister Twilight, follows her to earth, and is doomed to sink into Night."

In Haleole's romance there is a good deal of actual circumstance; he tried hard to make an historical romance out of the doings of mythical beings living in a mythical world; I have reshaped the story to bring out the fairy-tale elements that are in it. "The Princess of the Rainbow" is very much condensed from *Laieikawai;* the original is at least three times as long as the version given in this book.

THE FIRE-GODDESS

THIS is an outline of the story "Pe-le and Hi-i-aka" which Mr. N. B. Emerson published in Honolulu. Very fortunately Mr. Emerson wrote down this great piece of mythology while it was still living amongst the Hawaiians. What I give of this very dramatic myth is no more than an outline: Mr. Emerson's volume contains two hundred pages and one hundred and seventy *me-le* or dramatic chants are given in it.

THE SEVEN GREAT DEEDS OF MA-UI

THE number seven has no significance in Polynesian tradition; the number eight has. It just happened that the number of Ma-ui's deeds that had interest for me as a storyteller was seven. Fornander has only short and passing notices of Ma-ui, and all the material for the stories given here has been taken from Mr. W. D. Westervelt's valuable *Ma-ui the Demi-God*. Ma-ui is a hero for all the Polynesians, and Mr. Westervelt tells us that either complete or fragmentary Ma-ui legends are found in the single islands and island groups of Aneityum, Bowditch or Fakaofa, Efate, Fiji, Fotuna, Gilbert, Hawaii, Hervey, Huahine, Mangaia, Manihiki, Marquesas, Marshall, Nauru, New Hebrides, New Zealand, Samoa, Savage, Tahiti or Society, Tauna, Tokelau, and Tonga. Ma-ui is, in short, a pan-Polynesian hero, and it is as a pan-Polynesian hero that I have treated him, giving his legend from other sources than those that are purely Hawaiian. However, I have tried to make Hawaii the background for all the stories. Note that Ma-ui's position in his family is the traditional position for a Polynesian hero—he is the youngest of his brothers, but, as in the case of other heroes of the Polynesians, he becomes the leader of his family.

Ma-ui's mother was Hina. She is distinguished from the numerous Hinas of Polynesian tradition by being "Hina-a-ke-ahi," "Hina-of-the-Fire." I follow the New Zealand tradition that Mr. Westervelt gives in telling how Ma-ui was thrown into the sea by his mother and how the jellyfish took care of him. Ma-ui's throwing the heavy spear at the house is also out of New Zealand. His overthrowing of the two posts is out of the Hawaiian tradition. But in that tradition it is suggested that his two uncles were named "Tall Post" and "Short Post." They had been the guardians of the house, and young Ma-ui had to struggle with them to win a place for himself in the house. Ma-ui's taking away invisibility from the birds and letting the people see the singers is out of the Hawaiian tradition. So is Ma-ui's kite flying. The Polynesian people all delighted in kite flying, but the Hawaiians are unique in giving a kite to a demigod. The incantation beginning "O winds, winds of Wai-pio" is Hawaiian; the other incantation, "Climb up, climb up," is from New Zealand.

The fishing up of the islands is supposed by scholars to be a folk-lore account of the discovery of new islands after the Polynesian tribes had put off from Indonesia. The story that I give is mainly Hawaiian—it is out of Mr. Westervelt's book, of course—but I have borrowed from the New Zealand and the Tongan accounts too; the fishhook made from the jawbone of his ancestress is out of the New Zealand tradition, and the chant "O Island, O great Island" is Tongan.

The story of Ma-ui's snaring the sun is Hawaiian, and the scene of this, the greatest exploit in Polynesian tradition, is on the great Hawaiian mountain Ha-le-a-ka-la. The detail about the nooses of the ropes that Ma-ui uses—that they were made from the hair of his sister—is out of the Tahitian tradition as given by Gill.

The Hawaiian story about Ma-ui's finding fire is rather tame; he forces the alae or the mud hen to give the secret up to him. I have added to the Hawaiian story the picturesque New Zealand story of his getting fire hidden in the nails of his ancestress in the lower world. There is an Hawaiian story, glanced at by Fornander, in which Ma-ui obtains fire by breaking open the head of his eldest brother.

The story of Ma-ui and Kuna Loa, the Long Eel, as I give it, is partly out of the Hawaiian, partly out of the New Zealand tradition, and there is in it, besides, a reminiscence of a story from Samoa. All of these stories are given in Mr. Westervelt's book. That Kuna Loa tried to drown Ma-ui's mother in her cave—that is Hawaiian; that Hina was driven to climb a breadfruit tree to get away from the Long Eel—that is derived from the Samoan story. And the transformation of the pieces of Kuna Loa into eels, sea monsters, and fishes is out of the New Zealand tradition about Ma-ui. "When the writer was talking with the natives concerning this part of the old legend," says Mr. Westervelt, "they said, 'Kuna is not a Hawaiian word. It means something like a snake or a dragon, something we do not have in these islands.' This, they thought, made the connection with the Hina legend valueless until they were shown that Tuna (or Kuna) was the New Zealand name of the reptile which attacked Hina and struck her with his tail like a crocodile, for which Ma-ui killed him. When this was understood, the Hawaiians were greatly interested to give the remainder of the legend, and compare it with the New Zealand story." "This dragon," Mr. Westervelt goes on, "may be a remembrance of the days when the Polynesians were supposed to dwell by the banks of the River Ganges in India, when crocodiles were dangerous enemies and heroes saved families from their destructive depredations." Mrs. A. P. Taylor of Honolulu writes me in connection with this passage: "There is a spring in the Palama district in Honolulu called Kuna-wai ('Eel of Water'). In Hawaiian, kuna-kuna means eczema, a skin disease."

The story of the search that Ma-ui's brother made for his sister is from New Zealand. Ma-ui's brother is named Ma-ui Mua and Rupe. His sister is Hina-te-ngaru-moana, "Hina, the daughter of the Ocean."

The splendidly imaginative story of how Ma-ui strove to win immortality for men is from New Zealand. The Goblin-Goddess with whom Ma-ui struggles is Hina-nui-te-po, "Great Hina of the Night," or "Hina, Great Lady of Hades." According to the New Zealand mythology she was the daughter and the wife of Ka-ne, the greatest of the Polynesian gods. There seems to be a reminiscence of the myth that they once possessed in common with the New Zealanders in the fragmentary tale that the Hawaiians have about Ma-ui striving to tear a mountain apart. "He wrenched a great hole in the side. Then the e-le-pa-io bird sang and the charm was broken. The cleft in the mountain could not be enlarged. If the story could be completed it would not be strange if the death of Ma-ui came with his failure to open the path through the mountain." So Mr. Westervelt writes.

The Ma-ui stories have flowed over into Melanesia, and there is a Fijian story given in Lorimer Fison's *Tales of Old Fiji*, in which Ma-ui's fishing is described. Ma-ui, in that story, is described as the greatest of the gods; he has brothers, and he has two sons with him. With his sons he fishes up the islands of Ata, Tonga, Haabai, Vavau, Niua, Samoa, and Fiji. Ma-ui's sons depart from the Land of the Gods and seize upon the islands that their father had fished up. Then Disease and Death come to the islands that the rebel gods, Ma-ui's sons, have seized. Afterward Ma-ui sent to them "some of the sacred fire of Bulotu."

THE ME-NE-HU-NE

THE account of the Me-ne-hu-ne that I give is taken from William Hyde Rice's *Hawaiian Legends*, published by the Bishop Museum and Thomas Thrumm's *Stories of the Menehunes*, published by A. C. McClurg & Co., Chicago. I have treated this group as if the stories were being told to a boy by an older Hawaiian, and have imagined them both as being with a party who had gone into the highlands to cut sandalwood. As the party goes down the mountainside the boy gathers the ku-kui or candle nuts for lighting the house at night. The name Me-ne-hu-ne is applied in Tahiti to the lowest class of people, and in the Fornander Collection the name is used as implying the very early people of the islands.

THE CANOE OF LAKA OR RATA AND THOSE WHO SAILED IN IT

RATA appears as the ancestor of many of the Polynesian clans, and scholars are of the opinion that he is to be regarded as an historical character belonging to the time of the migrations that led to the colonization of the outlying islands; his contests with sea-monsters are to be regarded as mythical renderings of his struggles with storms, earthquakes, and human enemies. The story of the making of his great ocean-going canoe with supernatural help is the most widespread of the Rata or Laka stories; it is the Me-ne-hu-ne who build the canoe for him in Hawaii, and in the Southern Islands it is the gods. Did the South Sea Islanders who came to Hawaii with the whalers give the Hawaiians the Rata or Laka stories, or do they belong to the time of the undivided Polynesian group? I asked Miss Beckwith which was the most likely period for their distribution; she pointed out that incidents of the Laka stories have very definite locations on the Hawaiian Islands; this suggests that they have antiquity there.

The story about Rata that is given here was published by Mr. Stephen Savage in the *Journal of the Polynesian Society*, Vol. XIX. The stories about this hero that Mr. Savage has collected have much more of the grandeur of primitive myth than have any of the other stories about him. One feels in them the terror of the ocean and the mystery of islands come to for the first time. Who is Puna whom Rata in this story goes forth to take vengeance on? His children are Octopus, Clam, Great Shark; he is weak when "the cold south wind blows," and he is tied by his hands and feet to the trees and rocks. In a Tongan story a youth comes to an island that the Wind has possession of; he meets the Daughter of the Wind, and she ties her father so that he is not able to harm the youth. Is Puna, who can be tied up, the Wind? Or rather, is he Great Storm? Apa-kura, the wife of the chief who destroyed Rata, is a well-known personage in Samoan tradition. The New Zealand storytellers did not know that Rata's canoe had been turned into stone; in a story given by Sir George Grey, when Whaka-tau would go to make war for Hina and Tini-rau, he speaks of sailing in the canoe "of Rata, our ancestor."

WHEN THE LITTLE BLOND SHARK WENT VISITING

RETOLD from story given in Thomas Thrumm's *More Hawaiian Folk-tales*, with title "Story of Ka-ehu-iki-mano-o-puu-loa." A note says that the version given is a condensed translation from the newspaper *Au Okoa*, November 24, 1870.

THE BOY PU-NIA AND THE KING OF THE SHARKS

GIVEN in the Fornander Collection of Hawaiian Antiquities and Folk-lore, Memoirs of the Bernice Pauahi Bishop Museum of Polynesian Ethnology and Natural History, Vol. V, Part II, with the title *Kaao no Punia*, Legend of Pu-nia.

Like many another Polynesian hero, Pu-nia had a mother whose name was Hina. The shark's name, Kai-ale-ale, means "sea in great commotion." But the kindling of the fire inside the shark with the fire sticks could not have been so easy as it is made to appear. Melville, in *Typee*, describes the operation of fire-making as laborious. This is how he saw it being done:

"A straight, dry, and partly decayed stick of the hibiscus, about six feet in length, and half as many inches in diameter, with a smaller bit of wood not more than a foot long, and scarcely an inch wide, is as invariably to be met with in every house in Typee as a box of lucifer matches in the corner of the kitchen cupboard at home. The islander, placing the larger stick obliquely against some object, with one end elevated at an angle of forty-five degrees, mounts astride of it like an urchin about to gallop off upon a cane, and then, grasping the smaller one firmly in both hands, he rubs its pointed end slowly up and down the extent of a few inches on the principal stick, until at last he makes a narrow groove in the wood, with an abrupt termination at the point farthest from him, where all the dusty particles which the friction creates are accumulated in a little heap.

"At first Kory-Kory goes to work quite leisurely, but gradually quickens his pace, and waxing warm in the employment, drives the stick furiously along the smoking channel, plying his hands to and fro with amazing rapidity, the perspiration starting from every pore. As he approaches the climax of his effort, he pants and gasps for breath, and his eyes almost start from their sockets with the violence of his exertions. This is the critical stage of the operation; all his previous labours are vain if he cannot sustain the rapidity of the movement until the reluctant spark is produced. Suddenly he stops, becomes perfectly motionless. His hands still retain their hold of the smaller stick, which is pressed convulsively against the farther end of the channel among the fine powder there accumulated, as if he had just pierced through and through some little viper that was wriggling and struggling to escape from his clutches. The next moment a delicate wreath of smoke curls spirally into the air, the heap of dusty particles glows with fire, and Kory-Kory, almost breathless, dismounts from his steed."

OWL AND RAT AND THE BOY WHO WAS GOOD AT SHOOT-ING ARROWS

THE introductory story about Owl and Rat is given in *Folk Tales from Hawaii*, edited by Martha Warren Beckwith. The main story is given in the Fornander Collection, Vol. IV, Part III, of the Memoirs of the Bernice Pauahi Bishop Museum, with the title *Kaào no Pikoiakaalala*, Legend of Pikoiakaalala.

His father was Raven or Crow, his sisters were Rat and Bat. The arrows that Pi-ko-i shot were not from the sort of bow that we are familiar with; the Hawaiian bow, it must be noted, was not a complete bow. The string hung untied from the top of the shaft; the shooter put the notch of the arrow into the hanging string, whipped forward the shaft, and at the same time cast the arrow, which was light, generally an arrow of sugarcane. The arrow was never used in war; it was used in sport—to shoot over a distance, and at birds and at rats that were held in some enclosure. The bird that cried out was evidently the e-le-pa-io. "Among the gods of the canoe-makers," says Mr. Joseph Emerson, "she held the position of inspector of all *koa* trees designed for that use." The Hawaiian interest in riddles enters into Pi-ko-i's story.

THE STORY OF MO-E MO-E: ALSO A STORY ABOUT PO-O AND ABOUT KAU-HU-HU THE SHARK-GOD, AND ABOUT MO-E MO-E'S SON, THE MAN WHO WAS BOLD IN HIS WISH

THE story of O-pe-le, who came to be called Mo-e Mo-e, is given in the Fornander Collection, Vol. V, Part I, of the Memoirs of the Bernice Pauahi Bishop Museum, with the title *He Kaao no Opelemoemoe*, Legend of Opelemoemoe; the story about Po-o is given in the Memoirs of the Bernice Pauahi Bishop Museum, Vol. V, Part III (the stories in this volume do not belong to the Fornander Collection); the story about the Shark-God is taken from an old publication of the islands, the *Maile Quarterly;* the story of The Man Who Was Bold in His Wish is given in the Fornander Collection, Vol. IV, Part III, of the Memoirs of the Bernice Pauahi Bishop Museum, with the title *Kaao no Kalelealuaka a Me Keinohoomanawanui*, the Legend of Kalelealuaka and Keinohoomanawanui.

THE STORY OF HA-LE-MA-NO AND THE PRINCESS KAMA

GIVEN in the Fornander Collection, Vol. V, Part II, of the Memoirs of the Bernice Pauahi Bishop Museum, with the title *Kaao no Halemano*, Legend of Ha-le-ma-no.

Kama, or, to give her full name, Kamalalawalu, was living under a strict *tapu*. Ha-le-ma-no is no thoughtless *tapu* breaker, as are other young men in Hawaiian romance; there is very little of the mythical element in this story; the enchantress sister, however, is a figure that often comes into Hawaiian romance. This story is remarkable for its vivid rendering of episodes belonging to the aristocratic life—the surf riding, surely the greatest of sports to participate in, as it is the most thrilling of sports to watch; the minstrelsy; the gambling. The poems that Ha-le-ma-no and Kama repeat to each other are very baffling, and are open to many interpretations. In this respect they are like most Hawaiian poetry, which has a deliberate obscurity that might have won Mallarmé's admiration.

"COMPANION-IN-SUFFERING-IN-THE-GLADE"

GIVEN in the Fornander Collection of Hawaiian Antiquities and Folk-lore, Memoirs of the Bernice Pauahi Bishop Museum of Polynesian Ethnology and Natural History, Vol. IV, Part III, with the title *Kaao no Hoamakeikekula (Legend of Hoamakeikekula)*.

THE ARROW AND THE SWING

THIS is one of the most famous of the Hawaiian stories. It is given in the Fornander Collection, Vol. V, Part I, of the Memoirs of the Bernice Pauahi Bishop Museum, with the title *He Kaao no Hiku a me Kawelu*, the Legend of Hi-ku and Ka-we-lu. It should be remembered that Hi-ku's arrow was more for casting than for shooting: the game that he was playing at the opening of the story consisted in casting his arrow, *Pua-ne*, over a distance. Ka-we-lu was living under *tapu*. But, like many another heroine of Polynesian romance, she was not reluctant about having the tapu broken. There is one very puzzling feature in this story. Why did Ka-we-lu not give her lover food? Her failure to provide something for him is against all traditions of Hawaiian hospitality. Of course, in the old days, men and women might not eat together; Ka-we-lu, however, could have indicated to Hi-ku where to go for food. The food at hand might have been for women only, and tapu as regards men. Or it might have been tapu for all except people of high rank. If this was what was behind Ka-we-lu's inhospitality it would account for a bitterness in Hi-ku's anger—she was treating him as a person of a class beneath her. But these are guesses merely. I have asked those who were best acquainted with the Hawaiian tradition to clear up the mystery of Ka-we-lu's behavior in this particular, but they all confessed themselves baffled by it. The poems that Ka-we-lu chants to Hi-ku, like the poems that Ha-le-ma-no chants to Kama, have a meaning beneath the ostensible meaning of the words.

With regard to Ka-we-lu's death it should be remembered that according to Polynesian belief the soul was not single, but double. A part of it could be separated or charmed away from the body; the spirit that could be so separated from the body was called *hau*. In making the connection between Hi-ku and the lost Ka-we-lu I have gone outside the legend as given in the Fornander Collection. I have brought in Lo-lu-pe, who finds lost and hidden things. This godling is connected with the Hi-ku-Ka-we-lu story through a chant given by Dr. Nathaniel Emerson in his notes to David Malo's *Hawaiian Antiquities*.

Mr. Joseph Emerson gives this account of *Lua o Milu*, the realm of *Milu*, the Hawaiian Hades: "Its entrance, according to the usual account of the natives, was situated at the mouth of the great valley of Waipio, on the island of Hawaii, in a place called Keoni, where the sands have long since covered up and concealed from view this passage from the upper to the nether world." Fornander says that the realm of Milu was not entirely dark. "There was light and there was fire in it." The swing chant that I have given to Hi-ku does not belong to the legend; it is out of a collection of chants that accompany games. The Hawaiian swing was different from ours; it was a single strand with a crosspiece, and it was pulled and not pushed out.

Mr. Joseph Emerson, in a paper that I have already quoted from, *The Lesser Hawaiian Gods*, says that Hi-ku's mother was Hina, the wife of Ku, one of the greater Polynesian gods. In that case, Hi-ku was originally a demigod.

THE ROLLING ISLAND

THIS story is from William Hyde Rice's *Hawaiian Legends*, published by the Bishop Museum, Honolulu.

THE DAUGHTER OF THE KING OF KU-AI-HE-LANI

GIVEN in the Fornander Collection, Vol. IV, Part III, of the Memoirs of the Bernice Pauahi Bishop Museum, with the title *Kaao no Laukia-manuikahiki*. The girl's full name means "Bird-catching leaf of

Kahiki." Her mother is Hina, a mortal woman apparently, but her father is a demigod, a dweller in "the Country that Supports the Heavens." In the original, Ula the Prince is the son of Lau-kia-manu's father; such a relation as between lover and lover is quite acceptable in Hawaiian romance. When she comes into her father's country the girl incurs the death penalty by going into a garden that has been made *tapu*. Lau-kia-manu, in Kahiki-ku, seems to have the role of Cinderella; however, the Hawaiian storyteller gives her a ruthlessness that is not at all in keeping with our notion of a sympathetic character.

THE WOMAN FROM LALO-HANA, THE COUNTRY UNDER THE SEA

THIS story is taken from David Malo's *Hawaiian Antiquities*. A variant is given in the Fornander Collection. There are many Hinas in Hawaiian tradition, but the Hina of this story is undoubtedly the Polynesian moon goddess.

HINA, THE WOMAN IN THE MOON

THIS story is from Mr. Westervelt's *Ma-ui the Demi-God*. The husband of this Hina was Aikanaka.

THE TWO GREAT BROTHERS, NI-HE-U AND KANA

THE second of these two stories was heard by the Rev. Mr. Ellis a hundred years ago. "During our journey to-day we also passed another place, celebrated as the residence of the brother of Kana, a warrior; in comparison with the fabulous accounts of whom, the descriptions in the Arabian Night Entertainments are tame. . . . The tale which recounts his adventures, states, that the Hawaiians, on one occasion, offended a King of Tahiti; who, in revenge, deprived them of the sun; that after the land had remained some time in darkness, Kana walked through the sea to Tahiti, where Ka-hoa-arii, who according to their traditions made the sun, then resided. He obtained the sun, returned, and fixed it in the heavens, where it has remained ever since." Mr. Ellis goes on to say: "The numerous tales of fiction preserved by oral tradition among the people, and from the recital of which they derive so much pleasure, prove that they are not deficient in imagination; and lead us to hope that their mental powers will be hereafter employed on subjects more consistent with truth, and productive of more pure and permanent gratification." Here it is a retelling of "Kana, a Legend of Hawaii," given in

William Hyde Rice's *Hawaiian Legends*. I have expanded it so as to give the conventional adventures of the hero or heroine in the ascent to the world of the demigods—the adventures that Au-ke-le goes through when he is on the quest of the Water of Life, the adventures that Ta-whaki goes through in his quest for his wife, and the adventures that the youngest of the Maile sisters goes through when she would come to the house of her brother, Eyeball-of-the-Sun. Undoubtedly these adventures belonged originally to the story of Kana's quest, but Mr. Rice does not give them.

The first of these two stories is given in the Fornander Collection, Vol. IV, Part III, with the title *Kaao no Kana a Me Niheu*, Legend of Kana and Ni-he-u. Mr. Thrumm speaks of the legend of Kana and Ni-he-u as having "ear-marks of great antiquity and such popularity as to be known by several versions." The chant in which his grandmother prays for a double canoe for Kana is over a hundred lines long; Miss Beckwith speaks of this chant as being still used as an incantation.

AU-KE-LE THE SEEKER

GIVEN in the Fornander Collection, Vol. IV, Part I, of the Memoirs of the Bernice Pauahi Bishop Museum, with the title *He Moolelo no Aukelenuiaiku*, the Legend of Aukelenuiaiku.

Like many another Polynesian hero, Au-ke-le (to cut down his name from the many-syllabled one which means Great Au-ke-le, son of Iku) was the youngest born of his family. Fornander thought that his story "has marked resemblances in several features to the Hebrew account of Joseph and his brethren, and is traced back to Cushite origin through wanderings and migrations"—an idea which is wholly fantastic. The story as I have retold it is very much condensed.

Au-ke-le's grandmother is a mo-o—literally, a lizard. Dr. Nathaniel Emerson and Mr. William Hyde Rice translate "mo-o" by "dragon," and I fancy that "mo-o" created a sufficiently vague conception to allow the fantastic and terrifying dragon to become its representative. On the other hand, "dragon" tends to bring in a conception that is not Polynesian. I have not rendered "mo-o" by either "lizard" or "dragon." I prefer to let "mo-o" remain mysterious. Note what Mr. Westervelt says about the "mo-o" or "dragon" being a reminiscence of creatures of another environment.

The story of Au-ke-le is mythical: it is a story about the Polynesian gods. Au-ke-le and his brothers go from one land of the gods to another. The "Magic" that he carries in his calabash is a godling that his grandmother made over to him. There are many things in this story that are difficult to make intelligible in a retelling. It is difficult, for instance, to convey the impression that the maids whom the Queen sends to Au-ke-le, and her brothers too, were reduced to abject terror by Au-ke-le's disclosing their names. But to the Polynesians, as to other primitive peoples, names were not only private, and intensely private, but they were sacred. To know one's name was to be possessed of some of one's personality; magic could be worked against one through the possession of a name. Our names are public. But suppose that a really private name—a name that was given to us by our mother as a pet name—was called out in public: how upset we might be! Stevenson's mother named him "Smootie" and "Baron Broadnose." How startled R. L. S. might have been if a stranger in a strange land had addressed him by either name!

Later on Au-ke-le goes on the quest that was the Polynesian equivalent of the Quest of the Holy Grail; he goes in quest of the Water of Everlasting Life, the Water of Kane. The Polynesian thought that there was no blessing greater than that of a long life. There are many stories dealing with the Quest of the Water of Kane, and there is one poem that has been translated beautifully by Dr. Nathaniel Emerson. It is given in his *Unwritten Literature of Hawaii.*

> *A query, a question,*
> *I put to you:*
> *Where is the Water of Kane?*
> *At the Eastern Gate*
> *Where the Sun comes in at Haehae;*
> *There is the Water of Kane.*
>
> *A question I ask of you:*
> *Where is the Water of Kane?*
> *Out there with the floating Sun,*
> *Where cloud-forms rest on the Ocean's breast,*
> *Uplifting their forms at Nohoa,*
> *This side the base of Lehua;*
> *There is the Water of Kane.*
>
> *One question I put to you:*
> *Where is the Water of Kane?*
> *Yonder on mountain peak,*

On the ridges steep,
In the valleys deep,
Where the rivers sweep;
There is the Water of Kane.

This question I ask of you:
Where, pray, is the Water of Kane?
Yonder, at sea, on the ocean,
In the drifting rain,
In the heavenly bow,
In the piled-up mist-wraith,
In the blood-red rainfall,
In the ghost-pale cloud-form;
There is the Water of Kane.

One question I put to you:
Where, where is the Water of Kane?
Up on high is the Water of Kane,
In the heavenly blue,
In the black-piled cloud,
In the black-black cloud,
In the black-mottled sacred cloud of the gods;
There is the Water of Kane.

One question I ask of you:
Where flows the Water of Kane?
Deep in the ground, in the gushing spring,
In the ducts of Kane and Loa,
A well-spring of water, to quaff,
A water of magic power—
The water of Life!
Life! O give us this life!

The story of Au-ke-le has a solemn if not a tragic ending, which is unusual in Polynesian stories. Its close makes one think of that chant that Melville heard the aged Tahitians give "in a low, sad tone":

A harree ta fow,
A toro ta farraro,
A now ta tararta.

The palm-tree shall grow,
The coral shall spread,
But man shall cease.

KAULU, THE WORLD'S STRONGEST BOY

GIVEN in the Fornander Collection of Hawaiian Antiquities and Folklore, Memoirs of the Bernice Pauahi Bishop Museum of Polynesian Ethnology and Natural History, Vol. IV, Part III; also in Vol. V, Part II, with title *Kaao no Kaulu* (*Legend of Kaulu*).

THE TOGAN VERSE given with the dedication is by the Chief Tafolo; it has been translated by William Finau. It is proper to give the original in a volume that is of Polynesian interest:

Fakamolemole a houeiki mo ngaohi haa,
He oku mamao mo faingataa ae faanga;
Koe tolutalu nae tuu holo he ngahi halanga
Kuo fuu puli pea alu mo hono toutangata.
Ka ne ongo ene vao fihi mo tevavaa,
Kae fai pe ha vavaku mo sia faala
Kia Touiafutuna, koe uluaki maka
Nae fai mei ai hotau kamataanga.
Kehe koe talatupua ia mo fananga,
Oku utuutu mei ai sii kau faa.